GHOSTS in the VALLEY

The Return

Ghost Lore of

Muskingum, Morgan, Coshocton,

Guernsey and Tuscarawas

Counties, Ohio

And Beyond

GARY FELUMLEE

2018

Temple Party
October 26, 2018

Gary Felumlee

Dedicated to my father

Floyd Felumlee

who told me my first ghost story.

Table of Contents

Putnam Ghost Walk (M. Felumlee, 2017)

INTRODUCTION 2018

It has been nearly twenty years since my publication of the original **Ghosts in the Valley, Ghost Lore of Muskingum, Morgan, Coshocton, Guernsey and Tuscarawas Counties, Ohio**. Yet today, people still request copies of the original edition. Much has happened in the last twenty years and it is time for this update and expansion of the original work. There are new stories, updates to old ones and much interest in paranormal activity and investigation. The reader will find the original stories and a number of new ones too. Included in this publication will be highlights of numerous paranormal investigations that I have documented and been a part of since the first publication. Also included will be stories from a second publication; **Public Spirits of the Old Putnam District of Zanesville, Ohio** that I released as a self-guided walking tour in 2009.

The original format of stories is being maintained, along with the original print size. As in the original publication, there is a photo section included in the book. A major difference will be the inclusion of information my wife Melissa and I collected during our investigations with various groups and later with members of our own informal group, Spirit 7. I have maintained a record of our work through the years as individuals and in Spirit 7. So much has been there to discover and experience.

Looking back on twenty years, we see the explosion of interest in paranormal activity and for many; this includes participating in their own paranormal investigations. Television has increased the interest and even those that doubt the existence of "ghosts" have taken notice. Numerous locations offer opportunities for public investigations, from mansion houses, to old prisons and former asylums; they all offer the chance to experience the unexplained, the paranormal. There are numerous social media sites that draw interest and discussion of experiences. For the purpose of this publication, you may want to visit Gary's Paranormal Crossroads on Facebook. There you can even hear some of the "Ghosts in the Valley!"

In the "spirit" of this publication we will go back to 1998 and the original introduction. Soon our new journey into the dark corners, forgotten places and the world of spirit begins!

The subject of the ghost has been with us since the dawn of time. It appears in our oral traditions and our earliest writings. The ghost is always present. It lurks in the darkest corners of our mind and on the fringes of our physical and spiritual world.

It takes on many forms. A shape in the mist, a shadow in the hallway, a sound in the night, a light in the forest or graveyard, are all manifestations. Sometimes we smell or feel a presence. We often fear it as it intrudes into our lives and our mind.

What is a ghost? Is it the product of our imagination, the result of an overactive mind? Is it a piece of undigested food as Scrooge suggests in Charles Dickens' story *A Christmas Carol*? When we experience a ghost, does it provide us a glimpse of an existence beyond life as we know it? Could it be the leftover energy of a person's being or very soul? We do not have an answer. We can speculate from the rich traditions of the past or perhaps a future discovery may provide the answer.

Ghosts are often associated with events or locations. They seem to repeat the circumstances of their demise or often go about their business, oblivious to the startled onlooker. Are they caught in a time trap? Some ghosts have been known to interact with their human counterparts. Why are they different? One thing is certain, ghosts remain very much a mystery and maybe this is a part of their appeal. We love to listen to, read about, and hear their stories.

Tradition, dating back to the early 1800's and probably much earlier, states that a ghost may appear to warn the living of trouble. Sometimes it appears as if it has unfinished business on earth. The ghost is also said to appear when a living being meets an instantaneous death. Modern thinking often attempts to explain the ghost as a form of residue energy or an invention of the mind. In fact the ghost may be one or all of these.

In this collection, I have brought stories together from historical, primary, and secondary sources. Some come as oral tradition, but most of the collection, directly from those who experienced the phenomena. In all cases, the individuals believed they witnessed an event that is not easily explained outside the realm of the supernatural.

For those readers who remain skeptical, enjoy the collection. It is part of a rich tradition that is Appalachia and our beloved Muskingum Valley.

Your journey begins here. Gary Felumlee; 1998 and 2018

The Blue/ Blood Moon of January 2018. Photo by Gary Felumlee

Chapter 1

TRADITIONAL STORIES FROM EARLIEST SETTLEMENT

The first stories were handed down, generation to generation. The origins are undocumented but the stories have been published over the years and most have appeared in the Zanesville Times Recorder, submitted by either Norris Schneider or the author.

The early settlers brought with them deep rooted beliefs in the supernatural. There were so many things that could not be explained. They saw lights in the graveyards, rolling balls of fire in the woods, and heard sounds at night during their lonely travels.

Death was a constant companion and with it came vivid images of what Heaven and Hell could be. The Devil was lurking in the shadows, just waiting for the unsuspecting soul. He was a trickster and was always trying to steer his victim from the righteous path to Heaven.

One of the common images of the ghost was the forever wandering, restless spirit. We now meet Moses Dillon.

Moses Dillon

Moses Dillon first came to the Muskingum Valley as a Quaker missionary to the Indians. It was at this time he first saw the beautiful falls of the Licking River, and the location that to this day bears his name, Dillon Falls.

By 1806 he had built a great iron furnace at the falls. A small village of workers developed and Moses Dillon and his sons soon owned all the land along the Licking River, from the falls to where it entered the Muskingum River. The Dillon "Empire" with its furnace, mills and other businesses made the family rich by early standards. Near the eastern end of their property holdings, they donated land for what came to be called the Old Quaker Burying Grounds. Many members of the Dillon family and their community rest there - one apparently doesn't.

Autumn nights along the Licking River and Old River Road produce some of the thickest misty fogs that seem to hang in the valley. Sometimes the fog was so thick that it would interfere with weekend football games at nearby Gant Stadium. On those nights, it is said the ghostly figure of an old man materializes at the Old Quaker Burying Grounds and begins a walk to the falls of the river. Moses Dillon is said to continue to inspect his landholdings.

His family faced disputes over bridge building and could not seem to sell the furnace or some of his landholdings, as he approached his final years. This likely led to many nights when sleep eluded him. His mind was restless and worried.

Near the present day site of Thomas Lumbertown, once stood a train signal tower. On the second floor level of the tower was a small office. Night after night a lonely watchman would sit at his post, controlling the railroad traffic in the Dillon Falls area. His job was routine but at the same time very important.

One dark night as he manned his post and monitored the train traffic, there came a quiet tapping on the window behind him. At first he thought little of it and went about his business. Tap, tap, again the sound came to his ears. Enough was enough, he thought as he turned to see what was outside the window. In turning, it occurred to him that no one could be outside his window as there was no place to stand.

His mouth fell open as he struggled to understand the image before him. There in his window was an eerie glowing face, the face of the long dead Moses Dillon.

The old man's eyes seemed to look right through the watchman. There was a curiosity in them. You see, at the time of Moses Dillon's death, the railroad was new.

The glowing face in the window faded and vanished in the night. The watchman never forgot the night Moses Dillon returned to Dillon Falls. He shared the story with my grandfather who told my father who in turn told it to me, my first ghost story!

If you visit the Old Quaker Burying Ground today, you will see a mound that was placed in the center of it with the remains of shattered and broken gravestones imbedded in it. This was a project of Larry Fulkerson and a number of volunteers. The ground was cleared, the broken stones recovered and placed so the area could be maintained for future visitors.

Dillon family gravestones were returned to the site, including the one that belonged to Moses Dillon. Does the restless spirit of Moses Dillon still walk about on an endless quest to maintain a watch on his land holdings? Only time will tell and what is time to Moses Dillon?

Stumpy, the Human-Faced Dog

The area around Norwich and New Concord was settled by many people from the eastern colonies. They followed Zane's Trace into the new land; a number of them had received land grants from service during the War for Independence from England, the Revolutionary War. They brought with them colorful beliefs in witchcraft and the Devil. "Stumpy" is one of the tales that warns the listener to beware of the price of doing evil. This is the first of three stories that have their origin in or near Norwich and Stumpy Hollow.

Travelers on the back-country roads and paths of the early 1800's had many perils to face. The Indians said that witches took the forms of owls and would fly through the night sky in search of souls to steal. Woe be to the unwary traveler who did not follow the morals of the Christian life.

Some said it was the Devil himself that began to appear about the countryside of Norwich and New Concord. A great black beast, with the body of a dog and the face of a human was said to chase after the horses and carriages. It would appear out of the darkness and run alongside the horse and carriage as if in a great race. The frightened animals would often bolt, giving the passengers the ride of their lives or even causing accidents.

In one terrifying incident the creature, smelling of burnt sulfur, leaped upon a wagon and sat on the seat beside the horrified driver. It then jumped to the ground and bounded off through a cornfield and entered the woods. The shaken driver vowed to never again be out past the hour when most God-fearing souls were safe at home in bed.

A Second Stumpy Story

Norris Schneider, in an article that appeared in the *Times Recorder* on October 31, 1976, makes mention of a "Stumpy" at Norwich, in Muskingum County. This time the creature takes on a totally different form. Once again the story takes place in the early 1800's.

One dark late evening, early in the last century, a country doctor was making his way home. His old horse plodded along a narrow path which passed the community burial ground. The doctor was tired and looked forward to getting to bed. He entered the narrow lane in the hollow near the cemetery. The tree branches leaned out as if trying to delay his journey.

There was a dull thud as if someone had jumped up behind him in the saddle. He turned to look and to his consternation and terror, there, behind him on the horse was a headless man! The old doctor leaned forward as far as he could, and urged his old nag to run.

As they passed the burial ground, the headless visitor vanished. The frightened doctor shared his story in town and was considered a laughing stock. One man declared that no "Stumpy" would bother him and that the story was a hoax.

He decided to recreate the doctor's ride. At midnight, he entered the hollow near the burial ground. Slowly the rider and horse approached the burial ground. All was quiet, save the sound of the horse's hooves.

Then, there was the sense of a presence. The man looked behind him and there was Stumpy. The man screamed and his horse broke into a run. As they passed the cemetery, Stumpy made his exit. From that time on the hollow was known as Stumpy Hollow.

In later years, a poem was written about the tale. It was entitled *The Legend of Stumpy Hollow*, after the more famous *The Legend of Sleepy Hollow* by Washington Irving.

Stumpy Returns

Stumpy Hollow was the scene of yet another incident in the 1930's. Nola Everley shared this story with me from when she was a young woman. There was again excitement over the strange happenings around Norwich and near the cemetery there. Fall had come to the area and the warmth of summer was fading fast.

It had been a dark and dreary rainy day and the ground was saturated with water as night fell. Soon, as often happens, a ground fog began to float up from Stumpy Hollow, past the burial ground and into the village. It would be a chilly, damp night but a good spooky one to take a walk with that special person. Two couples were out together and as they walked near the cemetery, something caught their ear. It seemed to come from the woods below.

It was the sound of muffled steps, faint but drawing closer. Was it a horse? Maybe that was the sound, or maybe someone's cow was loose in the woods. Who would be out after dark riding a horse anyway? Lots of thoughts crossed their minds and some began to become more sinister. One thing was certain; the steps were closer now, ever closer.

As they strained to see what had caught their attention, a shape began to form through the mist, a horse and rider, maybe. The figure approached rapidly from out of the hollow. It was a horse and rider and to their terror, the rider had no head! As it neared the cemetery, it vanished and all was quiet. Stumpy apparently found a horse and the couples not only found there could be a little romance in a late evening walk but a bit of excitement too, at least if you are near Stumpy Hollow.

Sticky

Wood Spirits are often thought to be in the realm of European fairy tales. At least one seems to have made its way to the Muskingum Valley.

The Old Bloomfield Road, called Liberty Street in New Concord, was an important north-south route in the county. Before the Civil War it was a route utilized by escaping slaves on the Underground Railroad. It was also apparently the site of one of the most unusual hauntings in Muskingum County.

Late one evening, many years ago, a man was making his way home on horseback. It was very late and very dark. He thought of the day's events and that he soon would be home.

The horse was plodding along when suddenly it froze in its tracks. The man felt the hair on the back of his neck start to rise. What was wrong? What was about to happen?

With the crashing of branches, a creature sprang from the tree above him and landed with a dull thud on the back of his horse. The man screamed as the horse bolted into a wild run.

There, seated behind him, and grasping his waist was the figure of a stick man, the body made of twisted vines, leaves and sticks. In terror, the man and horse raced for home, their unwanted passenger bouncing behind them. The stick fingers seemed to dig into the man's side. The harder he tried to push away his unwanted guest, the tighter it seemed to grasp at him. Then, in an instant, it was gone.

Swampy

Oral tradition places yet another strange creature in the vicinity of Norwich, New Concord and east toward Cambridge. It is said to inhabit swampy wet ground and the story may have its origin in wet areas where Pennyroyal or Marsh Mint was collected, possibly even sighted in an abandoned quarry near Norwich.

This large Human-like creature is described as covered with reddish colored hair. It has been with us, in our traditions, in one form or another for well over two hundred years and likely much, much longer. Locals called the creature; Swampy. The Lenape people call the creature Misinghalikun, the masked being, keeper of the animals. Most of us know the creature as Bigfoot.

There have been reported sightings, tracks, strange screams in the woods and thumping on trees but we have no remains or DNA that is not disputed. So does Swampy roam through our woods, hills and swamps? Tradition says it does, why so many stories? Science is not convinced. There is one other possibility that comes to mind. What about a spiritual creature? Someday we may have an answer. Until then, Swampy remains in our oral traditions.

Mary Kethum

An old graveyard sits by a lonely country road in an isolated part of Coshocton County, Ohio. I have not visited the place but it is said to once have been the final resting place of Mary Kethum. This oral tradition states that a woman, suffering grave loss in her life was so devastated that she went on a killing spree. She was arrested and executed for her crime. Before she died, she swore revenge on those who carried out the sentence and their children.

Each Halloween after her death, she would return to the land of the living to seize children who were out just a little too late. The children would not be found again. In those early times her ghostly reign of terror had to come to an end. Her body was said to be exhumed and beheaded. Further, the head had to be buried miles away in an unmarked grave. Some say her spirit still roams the streets and country roads, searching for her severed head.

Searching for information on this story as to the historical accuracy, I found nothing yet the story persists to this day. Does it have a shred of truth or was it simply a way to insure good behavior on Halloween night?

Chapter 2

HISTORICAL HAUNTINGS OF THE MUSKINGUM VALLEY

The stories that follow are often associated with historical places, events and tradition. They have been told by word of mouth for many years and some in one form or another have been published. Their origins occur in the eighteenth and nineteenth centuries. Where publications have been found, they will be listed. The reader may wish to investigate the other sources for more detail or sometimes different variations of the tale.

The Ghostly Rider from 1764

Colonel Henry Bouquet was a professional soldier working for Great Britain in the fall of 1764. He was chosen to lead an expedition against the Ohio Indian tribes following the frontier war known as Pontiac's Conspiracy.

The Indians had taken many prisoners in their raids into Pennsylvania and Virginia. Some prisoners had been executed or died but many were adopted by the tribes. This included a large number of women and children. Bouquet was to demand their immediate release and did so as he neared each village.

His army made its way west from Pittsburgh, finally camping near present day Coshocton, Ohio. There he waited as messages were sent out to villages known to hold captives. Native American families gradually brought in their now adopted children as well as their adult prisoners.

The camp spread out for several acres upstream from the present city, though it has been hard to pinpoint the exact location due to the lack of much physical evidence. Parties would travel to and from the camp, sometimes hunting and fishing or scouting the surrounding territory.

Apparently, at least one soldier remains there to this day. There is a reoccurring visitation on Millcreek Road that seems to confirm this. A ghostly rider is sometimes seen, wearing a military vest and coat with shining buttons. He wears a three cornered hat and the ruffles of his shirt can be seen at the end of his coat sleeves. He wears shiny boots and white gloves. The face appears shaded but present, as he sits atop a fine white horse.

The image appears on the road, in front of the unsuspecting driver and abruptly turns up a steep hill, only to vanish in the night air. Some say this is the ghost of Colonel Bouquet, inspecting his camp. Another possibility is that it is the reenactment of the last moments of another soldier, who strayed from the camp and was found murdered and scalped.

In a bizarre twist to this story, the rider has also been reported as appearing without his head and carrying the hat in his hand. The haunting occurs near the Walhonding River, not far from its eastern bank, within about one-half mile of where the Muskingum River begins.

For more information on this and other hauntings in the Coshocton area, see Helen Meredith's booklet, *Ghosts!*

Mollies Rock

Mollies Rock is located in northern Muskingum County, Ohio. It stands in a beautiful setting of trees with a small stream running below it. One early story as to how it got its name goes back to the period when Muskingum County was a part of the frontier of the Ohio Country.

The story is one of forbidden love. It appears that a young woman was captured and adopted by the Indians. She soon found she was to marry one of the men in the village. She could not accept her fate, possibly because she was promised to someone at home or she simply could not adjust to the Native American lifestyle.

In her angst, she fled the village, and was pursued to the edge of the great rock. With nowhere left to run, she flung herself from the rock that bears her name. It is said that the sound of a sobbing young woman is heard above the cliff and a light is seen to fall to the creek below.

A more sinister story from the area is that the spirit of a young man, who committed suicide, stands at the edge of a cliff and attempts to coax others to join him.

A final story about Mollies Rock speaks of a peddler who was passing through the country one evening. As he approached the rock, strange noises seemed to echo from its surface, a low moaning like sound reached his ears, along with the clanking of an old bell. What evil lurked on the road before him? What terror awaited him in the darkness? It turned out to be the farmer's cow, and her name was Molly!

If one visits the rock today you will find a carving of a horse and a man with a hat, above the cliff face. The carvings are of unknown age and origin.

This site can be slippery and hazardous. It is not recommended that one attempt to walk near the edge of the cliff at any time.

The Falling Lights on the River

On some of the earliest maps of the Ohio Country, the Tuscarawas River, which helps to form the Muskingum River, is called the Muskingum River. The following story and the one that comes after it are from this part of the Muskingum Valley. Both occur in the 1700's.

In the 1770's, a Mingo Indian chief was said to marry a white captive. They started their life together and for a while it was one of happiness. The Mingo, because of his status, often traveled from one village to another. He attended treaty meetings and eventually converted to Christianity.

During one of his trips, he came upon a young Indian maiden, who fell in love with him. She threw her affections at him and he fell for her beauty. He took her as his second wife.

Somewhere along the river near New Philadelphia, the devastated and enraged first wife found the loving couple. Her jealousy reached its peak as she screamed and charged at the couple. The Mingo chief was caught by surprise and in an instant was knocked from the top of a high precipice. He plunged downward toward certain death.

His young Indian wife was caught in a death struggle with the enraged white woman. The first wife's strength was too much and the Indian found herself on the verge of falling. As the last inch of soil slipped from her feet, she grabbed her attacker in a death grip. Both sailed through the night air to their deaths, amongst the rocks on the edge of the river. The bodies were returned to the Christian Indian settlements, but were denied burial due to the circumstances of their deaths.

Soon thereafter, swirling, dancing lights were seen at the top of the cliff. Two were red and one was white. Shortly after they appeared, they were seen to plunge into the river and go out. This display is said to continue to this day and remind the viewer of love once gained and then lost forever.

For more information on this and other stories, see *Haunted Ohio* by Chris Woodward. It is on the recommended reading list at the end of this volume.

Ann Charity

Ann Charity was considered a frontier witch. She was a child of the frontier Indian Wars. The wars created her and her madness. She cast spells and made medicines. It was said she had powers over the dead. Her world was a mixture of Christian and Pagan religion. She was widely known and feared.

In 1782, the Christian Indians at Ganadenhutten were murdered, butchered, having their skulls crushed by wooden mallets. The Pennsylvania Militia attempted to kill every man, woman, child and infant in their hands. The blood and gore was said to drip from their fingers and smear their faces. Many laughed and swore as they attempted to burn the bodies. Later they bragged about their brutal acts.

The Indians began to raid the frontier in revenge and another army, under Colonel William Crawford went west into the Ohio Country. Many of the men had been part of the earlier party and looked forward to a fight.

The army camped in the valley of the Tuscarawas and Crawford was said to have a dream about his coming death by torture. In the same dream, Ann Charity was said to appear with an army of skeletons, marching toward Sandusky.

Crawford's army moved west and a vicious battle was fought, filled with hate on both sides. The Indians won a great victory and Colonel Crawford was captured and on the day of his execution he was stripped of his cloths, tied to a stake with a tether that allowed him to move about inside a circle of piled wood, shot by muskets only loaded with burning black powder, cut and slowly burnt to death, a gruesome execution. It was revenge for Gnadenhutton, an incident he had had no part in.

Straggling survivors of Crawford's army, made their way home as best they could, many again camping in the Tuscarawas Valley. In the night, a great thunderstorm hit the camp. In the flashes of lightning that appeared as hellfire, Ann Charity and her skeleton army passed the camp. Each carried on a pole, the bloody, dripping scalp of a soldier.

It is said her army reached the site of Gnadenhutten. The scalps were presented to the spirits of the murder victims and then cast to the wolves. The innocent people had been avenged.

Ann Charity, in her later years, resided at the Prophet's Town on the Ohio-Indiana border. She advocated only peace and was said to be living a Christian life. Tecumseh was away from the village, working to unite the tribes when death came to Ann Charity. Tecumseh's brother, the Prophet was at the village and he began to fear Ann Charity was a threat to his power. He ordered Ann Charity burned at the stake for witchcraft.

Shortly thereafter, General Harrison's army arrived and camped just outside the village, perhaps to provoke an attack. The Prophet, in his pride, attacked the army. The result was that his warriors were crushed, and the village was burnt. Never again was Tecumseh able to unite many of the Native American tribes, his credibility was shattered by the actions of his brother. Ann Charity finally appears to have found peace, though some will tell you her spirit still roams through the land she once called home.

Ann Charity's story can be found in a somewhat different historical format in Paul Kaufman's *Indian Lore of the Muskingum Headwaters of Ohio*.

The Devil Claims His Own

One of the stories often repeated in the traditions of Appalachia and the United States is the account where the Devil makes an intrusion in our lives to claim a soul. Our example takes place in northern Muskingum County or possibly Coshocton County, Ohio.

A man, many years ago lived a life of sin. He swore oaths, cursed and drank in excess. The one trait his neighbors feared most of all was his habit of challenging the Devil to take his soul. It was obvious he feared neither God nor Man nor Satan.

One fall night at a church social function, he made his appearance. In a drunken state he screamed for the Devil to take him. He laughed as his neighbors looked on in horror.

The night was dark as the man made his way home on horseback. As he approached the house, a large black form appeared in the road. As he drew closer, the man saw it was a great black dog.

The dog's eyes glowed and saliva dripped from its great mouth. For a moment, the great black beast and the horse and rider faced off in the road. In an instant, the dog lunged forward, the horse reared and the man fell from its back. There was a crushing sound as the man's head hit a fence post.

All was silent, as the dog began to devour the lifeless body. The Devil had claimed one of his own.

Dudley Woodbridge's Warehouse

Dudley Woodbridge was a merchant in the early years of Ohio. In the early 1800's he maintained a warehouse in Marietta and shipped goods on the Muskingum River to trading posts and stores upriver. His business was prosperous and a center of activity in the community. If you were to travel upriver or to the Salt Works at Chandlersville, Ohio, you likely would pay a visit to his store. Today, his warehouse is the oldest surviving structure of the original Marietta Waterfront, and upon my last visit, was serving as an inviting restaurant, overlooking the beautiful Ohio River.

Later in the 1800's it was part of a river city environment. There were numerous bars, taverns and houses of prostitution. The area, like so many such towns was often flooded, damages were sometimes heavy and soon the area became only a shadow, a memory of its once proud self. By then, the warehouse was a part of a small hotel or boarding house. It was often frequented by prostitutes and their customers.

There is a reoccurring haunting that is said to take place in the old warehouse, it happens along a stairway that leads to the second floor and involves a tragic murder.

A young man living in Marietta saw that his family seemed to be falling apart. His father was rarely home and his mother seemed to be in declining health. The young man felt helpless and angry, how could his father be so inconsiderate of the rest of his family? Why did he treat them like this? What had they done?

Word came to him that his father was seen down on the riverfront in the company of another woman, at Woodbridge's old place, frequenting the hotel. The son was heartbroken, devastated and decided to check for himself. One evening as his father left, the son waited and then followed. He inquired of his father at the hotel and quietly ascended the stairs. He stood outside the door for a moment and then burst through the door! There was a desperate scream and a muffled sound and a clatter of steps as the young man fled the building. Soon after, he was arrested for the murder of his father.

As if frozen in time, it has been reported that phantom steps are heard on the stairs, and a muffled scream and sound comes from the room, where the father met his fate. Sometimes people and time are not so forgiving.

Marietta has many stories of hauntings and ghosts. See Lynne Sturtevant's book, *History and Mystery in Ohio's Oldest City.*

The Buckeye Belle

In the 1840's and 1850's, the Ohio River and its tributaries remained very important for transportation. Railroads were just getting established so the steamboat "packet" was the way to ship goods to distant markets. The steamboats carried mail, livestock, produce and passengers. Much of the stoneware produced in our area was shipped downriver, sometimes all the way to New Orleans.

The Buckeye Belle was such a steamboat. She went into service in 1852. The Buckeye Belle carried the mail from Zanesville, Ohio to St. Mary's, Virginia (now West Virginia), across from Newport, Ohio. Passengers often used the boat as it was known to make good time up and down the river.

On November 12, 1852, the Buckeye Belle was making its way upriver toward Zanesville. It pulled into the locks at Beverly, Ohio and was about abreast with the upper guard lock. Soon it would be on its way to Zanesville. The passengers looked forward to ending their journey in a few hours.

The engines were building up a good head of steam as the Buckeye Belle began to churn away from the locks. In the next instant an explosion of steam, fragmented metal and fire rocked the unfortunate riverboat. The twin boilers had exploded! The force of the explosion rocked the community and sent the boat's cargo and passengers in all directions. One man was thrown partly through the roof of a nearby building. The destruction was everywhere, and pieces of human flesh and limbs were scattered over a wide area. The Buckeye

Belle's safe was thrown some three hundred yards from the boat. Twenty souls departed this life in an instant and several more died of their injuries a short time later.

Thirteen were buried at Beverly and a monument marks their resting place. Do they rest or are they still attempting to finish their ill-fated last journey?

It is said that on misty, foggy, fall nights, the Buckeye Belle and its cargo of departed souls attempts to finish her trip. The sound of the boat's whistle is heard as well as the ghostly turning of her sternwheel. Sometimes the shape of a steamboat seems to form in the wispy mists that rise up from the river's dark waters.

William Lawrence and Company

Old Washington, Ohio today is best known as the home of the Guernsey County Fair. It is a sleepy little town, bypassed by Interstate 70 but was once a bustling town on the National Road. The Lawrence family settled in Old Washington, prior to the Civil War. The family prospered there and built three homes. William's house was the grandest of the three.

His house was built in 1857 and his brothers' homes were constructed shortly thereafter. The structures were in varying states of preservation by the 1970's. Each was said to be haunted, as many old houses appear to be.

The Dixon family bought the William Lawrence house. They began to carefully restore their lovely home. By 1979, unusual events began to take place, according to an article in the *Daily Jeffersonian* newspaper, dated October 25, 1994.

It began when Mrs. Dixon saw the lights go on and off in the living room. An investigation was in order. Mrs. Dixon, accompanied by her dogs, went toward the living room. Within about eight feet of the door, the dogs beat a hasty retreat. At almost the same time, the living room door flew open!

As she stood there, heavy footsteps came toward her and through the door! No visible being made itself known but a chilling cold passed her as the sounds passed through the doorway. For some people, that would have been "it" and the dogs would have had some company. It was disturbing, but certainly no reason to leave.

The Dixons continued with the restoration project. One day, Mrs. Dixon was working on a ladder; she spied a movement through the transom. There was a young black skinned boy, about ten years old. In his hands he held an old fashioned lantern. The boy vanished as Mr. Dixon came up from the basement with the base of an old rusted lantern. It matched the one the visitor had held.

At the time of the newspaper article, the Dixons had also noted the sound of breaking glass and the beautiful notes of a harpsichord playing.

Sometimes during restoration, it seems paranormal activity peaks in some households. The William Lawrence house has remained active long after the original family left the residence. What's a big house without a few extra visitors? The Dixons didn't seem to mind.

The Runaway

Just before the Civil War, Ohio was subject to the Fugitive Slave Act. The law made it illegal to aid runaway slaves. Prison time and stiff fines could be expected for anyone who broke the law.

This did not stop slaves from making their way north, nor did it stop those who aided them in making their escape to freedom. On the other side, bounties were posted, rewards for returning the "property" of the slave owners to their plantations, farms and homes. Though there could be serious danger, the Underground Railroad, a series of safe houses and buildings continued to operate very successfully in Ohio. Putnam, about fifty percent abolitionist, was a stronghold for this operation. "Conductors" continued to guide those who yearned for freedom and "station keepers" provided shelter, safety and food.

An old Black man had spent all of his life as a slave. He made a vow to himself that he would die a free man. So as many did, he ran off one night. Using the rivers and the stars, he followed the "Drinking Gourd" or "Big Dipper" north.

He hid in the woods, in cemeteries and under bridges. Sometimes a person would lend a helping hand and feed and shelter the weary old man. The elements began to take their toll and the man grew weaker and weaker. Sickness became his companion but his spirit was strong and he pushed on.

The runaway traveled up the Muskingum River Valley to Putnam. There, he was taken in by one of the station keepers and could go no further. He was fed and treated with every kindness but alas, it was too late, and he died in their care.

Now, what was the family to do with the dead body of a slave? If anyone found out, the news would spread through the village and charges could be filed. The old slave was secretly buried in the dirt basement of a stone building in Putnam. This may have been the Stone Academy or possibly James Madison School.

As he did not receive a proper Christian burial, his spirit was said to roam the streets of Putnam and haunt the place of his burial. Some say the waters of the 1913 flood freed the man's soul while others believe he walks the streets of Putnam, in modern Zanesville, Ohio, waiting for someone to show him the way to freedom.

In 2008, the Ohio Paranormal Seekers investigated the Stone Academy. My wife Melissa and I joined the investigation. As investigators sat in the darkness of the basement, near the crawl space in the front of the building, one investigator felt a tug on her cloths. Tiny pebbles came out of nowhere and pattered on the floor. An investigator asked, "Who's There?" the words in reply on the digital recorder, though faint, appeared to say, "Black Man". Was the voice that of the old man searching for freedom, or yet another refugee, from a time long ago?

The Attic Visitors

An old house stands on Woodlawn Avenue in Zanesville, Ohio. It is one of the grand old houses that were a part of the Village of Putnam, formerly called Springfield for the old spring that to this day flows from Putnam Hill. This Greek Revival House, with massive white pillars, marks one of the residences of the Guthrie family. They were once prominent merchants in that community but also strong willed Abolitionists and station keepers for the Underground Railroad.

Harriet Beecher Stowe, author of *Uncle Tom's Cabin,* remarked of Putnam, where her brother was a pastor at the Putnam Presbyterian Church; that the village was about half abolitionist in their views. New Englanders, many who settled in Putnam, opposed slavery in any form.

Over the course of one weekend, an African American family was concealed in the attic of the Guthrie house. Bounty hunters, intent on the family's capture, and the reward it would bring, had all but captured them. Now they were roaming the streets, in search of information.

As the slave family peered from their hiding place, they could see the men, on fine bred horses, prancing and trotting about the dusty village streets. This went on for the better part of the day but the wait extended well beyond that time. The bounty hunters were given a misleading tip, as they searched the old stone quarry on Putnam Hill. This led them away from the village but they could still be in the vicinity, so it was unsafe to move on. Every noise, every voice outside, could be those hunters. At least for now, the family was safe but the fear was almost unbearable. It was hot and dark and yet no one dare leave the room.

Finally after a couple of torturous days, it was determined that the family could move toward New Concord after nightfall. From there it was to Bloomfield on the old Bloomfield Road, today called Liberty Street in New Concord. Leaving there, it was eventually north to Lake Erie, a steamboat trip and finally freedom in Canada.

Today, on quiet nights in the house, it is said that you hear murmuring and hushed voices in the old attic. Sometimes a soft weeping is heard. Do the spirits of fleeing slaves still inhabit this old house? Perhaps they find it hard to give up on a family and place that was so important to them. Then again, maybe what is experienced is a residual energy, not unlike a photograph, that is imprinted now in the walls of the place that absorbed such emotion and fear so long ago.

The Buckingham House

Another Putnam residence associated with the Underground Railroad is located near the intersection of Moxahala and Muskingum Avenue. This expansive federal style house once belonged to the prominent Buckingham family, again early merchants in Putnam. This house, recently a learning center, was apparently another station. As with most such stations, things were kept pretty much a secret.

The back stairway door to the residence was left open and sometimes the children would hear hushed voices or quiet steps in the early morning hours. Food was sometimes left there as well. The children, despite how curious they were, were told to never go to or use that stairway and they obeyed their father and mother. The reason was that the Buckingham family reserved that space for weary travelers that found their way there as the first streaks of light began to glow in the eastern sky.

To this day; steps, unexplained noises and hushed voices are occasionally heard along that back stair. One thing is certain, the children did a good job obeying their parents and if asked if they had seen any escaping slaves, their answer could always be the same. "No sir, I didn't."

Chapter 3

CIVIL WAR HAUNTINGS IN THE VALLEY AND BEYOND

Though the Civil War was far removed from the Muskingum Valley, except in July of 1863, with the visit of Confederate General John Hunt Morgan and his raiders, the spectral word of that time is with us yet.

Many stories come from this violent page of the country's history. The emotion of brother against brother, family against family, and the threat of instant death, all may play a part. Hauntings are numerous at sites associated with the American Civil War.

This chapter contains local stories as well as stories from Gettysburg, Pennsylvania. The Gettysburg stories are faithful accounts of firsthand experiences of Zanesville citizens who visited the battlefield prior to the publication of *Ghosts in the Valley* in 1998 and since. Included will be some later investigation summaries from more recent visits.

As you explore this section, keep in mind the traumatic events and emotional loses. Many a young soldier left his home and family, never to return, in this life. The Union was preserved, the slaves freed, but the cost of the war lingered, long after smoke from the last rifle fired in battle, drifted into the air.

John C. Hazlett in Command

On April 15, 1861, President Abraham Lincoln called on men loyal to the Union to come to arms. He wanted 75,000 volunteers to put down the rebellion in the South. Within three days of this call, John C. Hazlett had raised a company of seventy Zanesville volunteers. The company made its way to Columbus, Ohio before heading south.

Captain Hazlett's men said he was his own worst enemy. In leading his troops, he always exposed himself to danger. He was a man who believed that to lead you must be at the front of your troops. His men loved and respected his courage. They would follow him anywhere.

The company saw its share of fighting at Stones River in Tennessee, December 31, 1862 through January 2, 1863. It was in the thick of the fighting, and it was at Stones River, a Confederate mini ball found its mark. Captain Hazlett was wounded but refused to leave the field and stayed with his victorious troops.

The battle over, he returned to Zanesville for a short time to recover from his wound. After a limited time devoted to recovery, he returned to the field. Apparently an infection set in and in one evening, Captain Hazlett went from a healthy looking man to a corpse. His body was returned to Zanesville and received a hero's burial.

The Hazlett family again suffered loss on July 2, 1863 at Gettysburg when John's brother, in charge of a battery of guns on Little Roundtop, was killed by a Confederate sniper from the Devil's Den as he stooped to aid a dying general, also shot by a sniper. The Union held that hill that day in 1863, a crucial part of the Battle of Gettysburg. The family was to hold another funeral.

The site of the Hazlett family house is now home to an abandoned church which serves as a Senior Citizens' Center on West Main Street in Zanesville. The Civil War period lives on at this location in the form of three apparitions and a series of unexplained events. Multiple witnesses have taken note of the strange happenings there.

Lights are said to go on and off by themselves as do stoves, and water can come on by itself. Once a tray of food was said to be lifted from the table by unseen hands and dropped. Cups have been observed sliding across tables in the kitchen area as well. It is as if the spirits are saying, "Take notice, you are not alone." In the past two years (1998 edition), ghosts have materialized on at least three occasions. The first was the image of an officer, in full military uniform, complete with sword. He was seen walking about a room, then vanishing in front of a startled onlooker.

Two young men were on their way to a food storage area of the Center when they had their experience. They noticed a glowing light, the color of lightning, and in it was the figure of a stout woman, in a full hoop skirt. The style they described was that which was popular in the Civil War. When the second young man turned on the lights in the storage area, the lady disappeared and the young men did too! Only they had beaten a hasty retreat to another room.

Finally, one winter's morning in early January, a gentleman in black mourning clothes was seen walking about the rooms. A worker followed him to inquire about his business. The man, taking no notice of the worker, exited the building. As the worker reached the front door, the gentleman was nowhere to be seen. Funny, there were no footprints in the new fallen snow either, to give even a clue to the man's whereabouts. He had vanished! His world apparently had crossed ours for but a moment. His visit will long be remembered!

Today, as one views the building from the street, there is little that would remind you of the house that once graced the corner, now incorporated into the church structure. The Hazlett family, as so many did, gave so much to preserve the Union they held so dear. At this location, this Civil War drama continues its long engagement.

The Wounded Soldier Boy

A story that has been told around the Zanesville area for a number of years concerns the appearance of a wounded soldier in an old one room schoolhouse. The location is just west of Zanesville on Route 40, the old National Road.

Most often the soldier is described as a very young man in a military uniform that suggests the time period of the Civil War. Once he was described as a soldier from possibly the Revolutionary War. In this account it was stated he may have had a three cornered hat.

The soldier is said to appear with his head bandaged and blood seeping through the right side of the bandage. He may have other wounds as well as he walks with a crutch. The specter appears facing the viewer and then vanishes in front of its astonished host.

Speculation is that this young man may have left school to go to the war. It was not that unusual for young boys to lie about their age to enter the service. Some boys entered the service as young as fourteen, as infantry. Some women even managed to sneak into the army as young men. Some followed their husbands but many were single. In at least one case, a captain took one of these soldiers as an orderly and tent mate. Before the war was ended the men joked that the army had a "new recruit" as the couple had a baby son!

This young man may not have survived his injuries and his last thoughts of this life may have been his school, or someone he left behind. Perhaps a loved one never knew what happened to him and today, he still attempts to tell others of his fate.

In a final note, I once was told that a sword was found that may be associated with this story. This was a number of years ago and long before this work was planned. The source of that information is lost.

This story; or one very similar to it, appears in Chris Woodyard's *Haunted Ohio*. The reader may want to investigate that excellent collection of stories.

Morgan's Lost Raiders

In July of 1863, the Civil War came home to Ohio. As in part a distraction, to draw Federal troops away from Lee's invasion of the North, which ended at Gettysburg, General John Hunt Morgan launched a raid into Kentucky, Indiana and Ohio. On July 19, 1863 the Federal troops catch up with Morgan at Buffington Island. Morgan loses most of his command; some 800 soldiers are killed, wounded or captured, nearly all in the last category. Morgan and the remainder, some four hundred troops in all likelihood, were forced north and east with the Union troops in pursuit of their quarry.

Early in the morning on July 23, 1863 General Morgan and the remaining Confederates arrived at Rokeby Lock in Morgan County. There was a short exchange of gunfire before Morgan crossed the river and one raider fell mortally wounded. He died as the raiders moved toward McElhiney Hollow. They left his body wrapped in a stolen quilt. The next day the pursuit caught up at Old Washington in Guernsey County. Four more raiders died and are buried there.

The raider who died in Morgan County was buried behind the farm in the hollow but some years later his body was disturbed and later moved. The four Confederates that died at Old Washington are buried in the cemetery that overlooks the town.

Some feel these soldiers still haunt the places of their burial. They cannot rest, longing to return home, back to family and friends they left so many years ago. Like so many of their comrades, both North and South, they remain a long way from home.

Gettysburg Experiences

Gettysburg, Pennsylvania is a long way from the Muskingum Valley but many soldiers from our area served there during the Battle of Gettysburg on those hot, humid days of July 1-3, 1863. Gettysburg is called the turning point of the Civil War. The North was now on the defensive as General Lee's Confederate Army invaded Pennsylvania. General Meade knew this battle could well determine the future of the nation.

The following stories round out and greatly expand the Civil War section of this work in 2018. The original stories are here, supplemented by summaries of investigations we have done as individuals and by members of our Spirit 7 paranormal investigation team. If you choose to investigate Gettysburg today, be aware of park hours but also know that early morning is nice in the park. Many locations outside the park are active as well. Gettysburg is certainly one of the most active places in America. Always respect the fact you are on a battlefield and respect those that gave their lives there.

Face to Face with the Past

The Battle of Gettysburg was the turning point of the Civil War. The South, by winning a victory might cause the North to ask for peace. For three days in July of 1863, the armies faced each other. The heaviest fighting of the second day centered on a boulder-strewn area referred to as Devil's Den and Little Roundtop.

Many southern lives were lost in the attempt to overrun the Union positions. Ultimately the attempt failed. The area was littered with dead bodies and today is considered one of the most haunted places in the battlefield park.

In early June of 1996, an Adult Education Class and their teacher visited the battlefield. Knowing of the ghostly reputation of the place, some of the students visited the battlefield at night. They met with limited luck.

However, on an early morning visit the luck changed! As the students visited the Devil's Den, the teacher walked down a nearby trail. He recounted the ghost story of a Texan that was said to appear there, as the teacher filmed the trail before him.

First, on his black and white viewfinder, he saw a shimmering light on the trail. As he talked and recounted the story, the light took the shape of the hat, head and shoulders of a scraggly bearded man. Its form shimmered in light as it faced the camera. After filming the event for a short time, the teacher put the camera on pause and cut the distance between himself and the face by half. The ghostly face vanished. Filming at a closer distance produced no image.

A month later, the teacher, his wife and a friend visited the same area, and the same exact spot. No image appeared. As they stood and discussed the incident of a month before, the smell of burnt gunpowder invaded their senses. This continued for as long as they stayed in that place. No source could be found and it had been, at that time, over 130 years since any fighting occurred there.

Time Marches Backwards

The Devil's Den, Slaughter Pen, and the Valley of Death are all located in the same part of the Gettysburg Battlefield. Very unusual experiences have taken place as one explores this part of the battlefield. Sometimes parts of the battle are said to reoccur, for the startled visitor.

In June of 1997, another class visited the battlefield with their teacher. Hearing about and seeing the tape of the incident the year before, the class was not to be denied. They chose to visit the same trail the teacher had visited the year before.

Two watches were set for 9:00 pm and the little group advanced into the darkening woods. They could hear the sounds of children playing at Devil's Den and the cars as they went by. As they reached a small rock covered stream, an owl called out over the woods. The teacher called back, thinking that the owl was probably a prankster. The owl returned the call but now, from a great distance. It was real.

At the small stream, a decision had to be made; turn back or continue on. It would soon be too dark to cross the rocks safely. The group continued to push forward.

Suddenly, all the night sounds went quiet. No children or cars could be heard. The little group hesitated and moved closer together. At a slow pace they continued forward. Some saw faint glowing lights, the form of an animal, maybe a horse or deer moved off in the distance. It too appeared to glow. The feeling one gets when you don't feel alone, began to make its way through the group. It was time to leave! They quickly found a side trail and made their way out of the creek valley, unknowingly following the same direction as the Confederate attack there on July 2, 1863.

Upon reaching the clearing, the snorting sound of a horse came to their ears. Then there was the faint clip clop of the hooves and the sound of saddle hardware jingling. Yet, no horse was to be seen.

Not until almost to the road did they again hear the night sounds of crickets and frogs and the children and cars. One student felt she had nearly stepped on a soldier's body and fled ahead of the others. Upon reaching the vehicle, the watches were checked. There was now a gap of twenty minutes between them and the second hand on one was running backwards.

As the students got back into the van, one, a sensitive, made a disturbing remark. "He's there, in the back of the van!" That ended our adventure for the night. The watch did not correct itself till sometime after we had returned to our relatively safe motel rooms but then, this is Gettysburg.

Pipe Smoke and Blankets

The Colton Motel in Gettysburg, Pennsylvania is located on the perimeter of the Gettysburg National Battlefield Park. It is an older motel and has been known as a place of ghostly activity. In fact, that was one of the reasons we picked it for an Adult Basic Literacy Education trip.

We had spent an enjoyable, but long day visiting the park, the wax museum and also some shops. We had been out on the field of battle but hadn't had any ghostly experiences though had learned a bit of history. It was about 10:30 pm when we returned to our motel and found we were sharing it with a beer drinking motorcycle club. They were loud but a friendly group and soon we settled into our rooms.

Two students had been trying to catch some E.V.P. (Electronic Voice Phenomena). It was dark and they were near the cemetery. They came back, only to find that in the darkness, they had hit the play button on their recorder but not the record button! Disappointed as they were, they had no desire to try again that night.

Soon it was quiet outside and a number of students had gotten ready for bed. They were playing cards, this group of young ladies, and discussing the adventures of the two who had tried to record the E.V.P. In their effort to get a recording, they had asked the spirits to join them.

As they discussed their efforts, the springs on a rollaway bed began to creak and the mattress to sag a little. There was a startled look from the card players! Now the room began to smell of old pipe tobacco smoke!

The youngest of the group jumped up, grabbed the blanket from the rollaway bed, wrapped herself in it and ran down to another students room. She had to tell her roommate what was happening. The roommate said, "No way, you guys are trying to scare me." The young messenger, in her excitement, left the blanket and returned to her other friends. It wasn't but five minutes until the phone rang. "It won't work; you just want to scare me! Who blew the pipe smoke in here?" There was a moment of silence, than the answer came, "No One!" "But there is no longer any smell up here!"

Sometimes, you get what you ask for, a friendly visit! That's the spirit.

Revisiting Pickett's Charge

July 3, 1863 was the third day of the Battle of Gettysburg and it determined the outcome and ended the advance that might have forced the United States of America to recognize the Confederate States of America as an independent nation. General George Pickett led the fateful charge, ordered by General Robert E. Lee, over General Longstreet's objections. The result, Lee's ordered attack cost the lives of hundreds of his soldiers. Often, there was only an instant separating life and death. Many Southerners would never see home again.

It was a great Union victory and at the same time, a dreadful slaughter of life. As the cannons fell silent and the acid smoke began to lift, the scene before the victorious Yankees was one of total destruction.

It was getting toward nightfall as we arrived at the site of the beginning of Pickett's ill-fated charge. We had been drawn to this place by stories of paranormal activity, concerning a spirit that was said to harass women as they walked on a path beside some trees. There were also reports of orbs, sometimes considered balls of spirit energy, being photographed near the Virginia monument. Knowing the history of this part of the battlefield, we thought it was a good spot to visit.

Our party of five, three women and two men had decided to visit the field in period clothing. Two of the women had purchased new Civil War Era dresses and wanted to wear them. This we felt might increase our chances of an experience as often things easily recognizable are said to attract the spirit world. We had taken a few photos and took some time to appreciate where we were.

It was getting darker and the evening dew would soon cover the high grass. The decision was made to advance into the field, toward the Union side of the field, about a mile away. We spread out in a line and began to move forward. Step by step we felt we were experiencing history. We moved forward over the darkening ground. I could imagine the high hopes of the Confederate soldiers as they started that charge on July 3, 1863.

We had gone forward some distance and left most of the other visitors in our rear. I was attempting to explain that at the point where we were, the soldiers would be receiving cannon fire from the distant ridge and that the rebel advance was to focus on a distant clump of trees. We continued to advance. There was a noise, almost like a whimper, to my left and behind me. I looked back and there stood our youngest member in her beautiful Civil War dress.

She was standing frozen, like one of those stone monuments, not a twitch of a movement anywhere. Her face seemed sculpted, her eyes looking off to a distant place or time. I spoke to her, no answer. I moved closer, took her arm and spoke again, no answer. I tugged her a little harder and moved her from the spot. She was quiet, not speaking at first.

Finally, as we gathered around her, she spoke. "It was the deepest sense of sadness I have ever felt. It was a desperate, a deep sadness, I couldn't move from it. It was cold, deep and so, so, sad."

We will never forget that evening in what some say is the most haunted place in America. Did this soldier live just long enough to know he would never see his friends, loved ones or family again in this life? Does he remind us of that desperate charge and the countless personal tragedies that occurred on that field so long ago? That night we truly experienced Gettysburg.

P.NOEL Rock

Some legends persist and seem to last even though conflicting stories exist as to their origin. P. Noel is one of these. One thing is a fact. P. NOEL is carved in bold letters on a rock above Devil's Den, in the New York artillery position, overlooking the triangular field. Often as not one will find a penny just above the deep carved letters.

A few years ago my brother Keith, his son Aaron and I went in search of the carving. We had originally read the story in Mark Nesbitt's *Ghosts of Gettysburg* series.

It was getting dark, near closing time and a bit brisk. We had just enough light to find the stone and examine the carving. The telltale penny was resting just above the name. We knew it was bad luck to take it or we had least heard it was. We took a picture of it instead.

Was this a carving left by a soldier? Was it the work of a tourist from years ago? Was it burned into the stone by the Devil? We had heard all of those stories. The lichens on the stone said it wasn't of recent manufacture. We settled on a fourth story. The stone carving was a memorial to "Penny Noel."

We began to recount the story of a beautiful young farm girl on a fateful wagon ride with her father. At first it seemed that we felt a presence. We continued on. The wagon hit a large stone in the darkness, propelling the unfortunate girl from her seat. As she hit the ground, the wagon's wheel passed over her neck, separating her head from her body, instant death.

The father was distraught; his beautiful daughter was dead.

It is said the young woman roams the nearby stream in search of her head. One can sometimes hear her as she wades about the stream. A moaning wind indicates she is with you.

As the story ended, as if on cue, a bone chilling wind kicked up. A faint moaning accompanied the wind as it worked its way through the trees. It was a long time ago. I snapped a parting shot of young Aaron and his dad. We have never forgotten our search for P. Noel. Some, including Aaron say we found her that night.

Sach's Bridge

Sach's Bridge was a key bridge during the Battle of Gettysburg. Both armies used it to move men, horses, wagons and weapons. It also served as a hospital for a short time. One story states that three rebel deserters were hanged at the bridge by order of their commander.

The bridge, located not far from the Esienhower Farm was a popular site for paranormal investigators after the battlefield park had closed for the night. Friends would congregate there and talk "ghosts." This was very popular the last time we visited the bridge, several years ago.

On any given night, especially the weekend, you might find people there from Pennsylvania, Maryland, New York, Ohio and other states. Most visitors hope for an experience as the bridge is known for a "hot spot" of activity.

Melissa and I arrived one night, in our Civil War reenactor attire. People told stories of lights moving along the creek, forms on the bridge and orbs of light, "spirit energy", being photographed. One person had their night vision infrared scope. I had my 35mm camera at the time.

We joined a group that ventured across the bridge for a walk up the lane. Earlier that night someone had seen a dark shadow moving in the field on the right. It was a human form but there was a sense of dread or evil some had experienced. The feeling was described as powerful and dark. After the battle, many wounded soldiers had been treated there and many had died. Some speculated this was the cause of the occurrence.

Our group didn't seem to contact anything paranormal and we made our way back to the bridge. Off and on we noticed a faint light some distance in front of us. It wasn't until we returned to the bridge that those who had stayed behind spoke up.

They had seen a guide leading our group. At first a person with a flashlight was suspected. Instead, our guide was a dark shadowy form that seemed to carry a lantern and was looking for something or someone. The figure never made it to the other side but faded as it came closer to the bridge.

Melissa and I mingled for a while at the bridge and the group dwindled over the next hour. It was approaching midnight and there were maybe a half dozen of us left at the bridge. I thought, let's try an experiment.

I asked Missy to go onto the covered bridge and come toward us in her Civil War dress. Missy came toward us, humming some Civil War music and swaying as though dancing.

The guy with the night vision scope exclaimed, "There's ectoplasm going onto the bridge!" With that I immediately took the picture. White columns of mist were surrounding Missy. What a night for a dance! So much can happen at Gettysburg.

The Crying Soldier

Baltimore Street in Gettysburg is one of Gettysburg's busiest streets. It features the "Diamond" a roundabout in the center of town. A friend recalled a story that seems to speak on a personal level of the last moments on Union soldier on the first day of fighting.

During the first days fighting at Gettysburg, the Union battle line finally collapsed and the outnumbered defenders retreated through the town. Some fighting was street by street and house by house. Sharpshooters on both sides took their toll, firing from some upstairs windows.

A young Union soldier was discovered in the upstairs of a house. It is not known if he was shooting or hiding. He surrendered and pleaded for his life as tears streamed down his face. The Confederates did not listen to his pleas and shot him to death on the stairway. His lifeless body fell to the floor below. Today he appears when arguing and fighting occurs at the house as if pleading for the fighting to stop, tears still flowing down his cheeks.

Into the Fields

Since the publication of *Ghosts in the Valley*, in 1998, Melissa and I, sometimes joined by members of our Spirit 7 team and other friends, have spent much time at Gettysburg. We go there for the history, to a place that in many ways determined the path of our country, even to the present day. We have spent hours doing historical research and hours in the field, including doing paranormal investigations. In this section the reader will find highlights of a few investigations.

It is very important to study areas of the field, as to what occurred there. We have found success in paying attention to details; names, states, regiments and results are all important. Soldier's accounts are good as are numerous publications concerning the battle. My favorite publication for a solid, quick reference is, *The Maps of Getteysburg, An Atlas of the Gettysburg Campaign, June 3-July 13, 1863* by Bradley M. Gottfried. It contains pages upon pages of maps and detailed information, essential for research and a good investigation.

For these investigations, we rely heavily on digital recorders of which I prefer Sony, though have used others with success. We also use Gauss meters, (EMF Detectors) but do not recommend the various "voice boxes" which go by various names, and phone applications that work radio bands. They are inconsistent in my opinion, and can lead the investigator down false paths. One should have some knowledge of the time period, the thoughts and ideas of the time. Knowing some of the music and some aspects of everyday life during the Civil War is good. Ask your questions and leave a few seconds for possible responses to be recorded on your digital recorders. We have often found that two digital recorders in our vicinity, though some distance from each other, can produce favorable results. We also use digital cameras and occasionally night vision equipment. To me, the E.V.P.(Electronic Voice Phenomena) you get on the recorders remains the most convincing evidence you get in a session. Finally be aware of physical experiences, most commonly a cold presence touching you. You may get a feeling of someone there with you and in some cases, experience a feeling of static electricity around you. Always use caution and avoid dangerous situations or locations. It is best to scout a site in the daylight for hazards. Take note of time restrictions and location restrictions should you choose to investigate a site.

The Brafferton Inn

The Brafferton Inn was built in 1786 by the Codori family. In early March of 2011 Melissa and I stayed there in the "Battle Room", so named as imbedded in the mantle of the fireplace is a mini ball from the first day's battle in the town. The room is located in the 1786 part of the house and we were the only guests in that section. The first evening there, we conducted a short investigation in our room. It was approaching midnight.

Activity began about twelve minutes into our questions. We heard a tap and recorded a faint female voice, though no one was in the building that night. There was another tap and I asked a battle oriented question at just over fourteen minutes into the session. I was talking toward the Union side.

Gary: "By late afternoon your line fell apart." The response (E.V.P.): "Wooo!"

Later we focused on the Codori family which had come from France and settled in Gettysburg. I asked if the family loved this house and there was a muffled response. Then I asked," Did you come from France?" "Yes" was the recorded response from a female voice. Knowing that the family had helped wounded soldiers after the battle at their church, I asked if anyone was still here, with us that had attended church after the "battle?" "Two" was the response, again apparently female. Finally, I asked what it was like on the "other side?" "Change" was the nearly inaudible response.

The next night we were joined by my brother Keith and his son Aaron. We again did a short investigation session in our room. At about nine minutes into the session we heard what sounded like faint steps on the stairway. I asked for anyone with us to give us a sign. I then asked, "Are you male?" There was a tap. "Are you a Union soldier?" There was a loud tap. Later we asked of slavery. There was a recorded response but faint and inaudible. About five minutes later we hear what sounds like furniture being moved in the next room. Upon checking this, we found no one. It had only been about twenty minutes and we were getting ready to go outside so I asked, "Do you want us to leave?" The recorded female response, possibly a child was "Uh Huh." I then asked, "Do you get up early in the morning?" A female voice answered, "Yes."

The Brafferton Inn Bed and Breakfast is a great place to stay and right in the center of town. Even if you are there in the off season, chances are you are not alone.

The Farnsworth House

The Farnsworth House was located near the front line of the Confederate force that occupied Gettysburg by the end of the first day's fighting. Snipers used its attic to harass Union positions above the town. In fact, at least one died there. The side of the building that faced the Union lines is pock marked to this day by Union mini balls, many of them.

Some say the house may be the most haunted in Gettysburg; it also serves a historic menu for dinner in a beautiful Victorian setting. It has been the site of Mourning Theatre for many years, and crowds often gather there to hear dramatic ghost stories and participate in ghost walks as well.

Farnsworth House is also a bed and breakfast. We stayed there over a weekend in the off season, in one of the rooms in the old section of the house. Again we found ourselves with the place pretty much to ourselves the first night of our visit though numerous people were there by the second evening. The rooms are beautiful, furnished with antiques and history comes alive in the place. We explored a bit that first night and decided to try an experiment.

Melissa and I had heard the tragic story of a young boy who died in the house after being run over by a horse drawn wagon. His playful spirit is said to inhabit the house and play tricks on unsuspecting guests. He is fascinated by coins, small toys and other objects.

Before heading to the historic Dobbins House and the tavern there, we set up an area for the boy to enjoy. We placed some coins, antique marbles and an old, small metal horse toy there at the bed. We also placed our E.M.F. detector there which lights up and makes a rapid beeping noise when spikes are detected in electro-magnetic energy fields. We hoped the boy; Jeremy, I believe was his name, would find the gifts and have fun with the flashing light and sound.

We left the room with a digital recorder running and our Sony Camcorder with its night vision feature on, recording a mini DVD. We went downstairs and locked the guest entrance and left.

After a fine dinner at Dobbins House and a little exploring, we returned to our room at Farnsworth House. We had no sooner left, within less than fifteen minutes and the camera had recorded the E.M.F. detector beginning to flash lightly and beep. Then all of a sudden the readings peaked and the light was flashing fast and constant and the individual beeps were blending together and intense. The energy was centered on the bed area!

This continued for several minutes and at times would ebb and flow in intensity, as if the energy was moving about the area. Otherwise the camera only caught some blurring but no real image or figure and what almost sounded like an electric-like voice on occasion. The recorder did not pick up any E.V.P. activity, though sometimes if one leaves a recorder in an active area it does collect voice recordings.

We feel that Jeremy or one of the other spirits that seem to call Farnsworth House home paid our room a visit that night. Never to this day have we recorded such intense E.M.F. activity over an extended period of time. We had a session late that night but nothing materialized though as we lay in bed, a couple of times the meter again announced we were not alone!

The Battle for Devils Den and the Triangular Field

On November 12, 2011, Missy and I were again in Gettysburg. We decided to visit the area of much fighting on the second day of the battle. From Devil's Den one looks over the "Valley of Death" leading up to the high ground of the "Roundtops." The right flank of anyone facing the "Roundtops," bends to overlook a slope strewn with boulders and a low stone wall. This area is known as the Triangular Field, and was the site of heavy fighting the second day. General Sickles had taken it on himself to occupy the area around Devil's Den and the nearby Wheatfield, extending the Union line beyond the initial high ground the Union Army held. He was in an exposed position and the Confederates took note of it.

The Confederate attack came in the afternoon and the area around Devil's Den was defended by the 124th New York Infantry and a little farther off, the 4th Maine Infantry. Smith's, battery, 4 guns of it, supported the Union infantry. The 1st Texas Infantry advanced to the Triangular Field for the Confederates. The area we were investigating was contested between New York and Texas.

We arrived at the Triangular Field at 5:30 pm. There was a lot of noise and kids playing at Devil's Den. We made our way downhill to a stone wall. We positioned ourselves to the left of center in a grassy area, facing down the hill. I proceeded to recount the events of July 2, 1863 at this location. There was at least one other investigation group about 100 yards from us in some woods.

We placed two digital recorders on the wall, maybe ten yards apart. We were closest to the recorder on the left as we faced the woods below. During the investigation we collected some minor E.M.F. hits but focused our attention on questions directed to both sides in the conflict. E.V.P. was collected from both recorders.

We got our first response on the more distant recorder, a male voice saying "Right". This was about six minutes into the session. There had been no direct question so maybe it was a response to my recounting the history.

Recorder one was to my left and close by while recorder two was on our right and we soon got responses on both.

Recorder 1: Any soldiers from the 124th New York, you may approach us here.

Answer: "Okay."

Recorder 1: This is part of the Triangular Field.

Answer: "Right field." (Possible New York Accent)

Shortly after that response, a photo revealed an orb beside me.

Recorder 1: Did this wall protect you for a while?

Answer: "Yes." (Low Voice, Faint)

Recorder 2: Smith's Battery, he was throwing everything he had at you.

Answer: "I know." (1st Texas)

Recorder 1: You drove the 1st Texas in front of you, is that true?

Answer: "It was."

Recorder 2: "Gettysburg"

Recorder 2: You guys know the war is over?

Answer: "Yes." (Faint female voice)

Recorder 1: Is there a message you want someone to have?

Answer: (Very faint, inaudible response)

Recorder 2: (About five minutes later)

Answer: "Hi" (Possible female voice)

Answer: "Yea" (Female)

Answer: A chuckle (Male)

As a final attempt at obtaining interaction, I sang a little Dixie and a little Rally Round the Flag, than we said the Lord's Prayer. We were at the site some fifty plus minutes and I closed the investigation with; "In closing, Blessings to All." At that point recorder two picked up a faint response, "Thank You."

The 1st Minnesota

Early one morning I decided to visit another site associated with the second day's fight. In fact it marked the end on the Confederate advance and helped secure the Union position for the night. The position was some distance from the present day road system but it seemed to offer an opportunity to investigate an area that was subject to few modern distractions.

It was late in the day on July2,1863. Wilcox's Alabama Brigade, four regiments, advanced on a gap in the Union line. The only troops General Hancock had to blunt the attack were the 1st Minnesota, and only eight companies of it. The Minnesota troops had watched the Union lines collapse and fall back; they didn't want to see a battle lost on Northern soil. They fixed bayonets and charged directly at the 10, 11, 14 and 9th Alabama Regiments. The front line of the Alabama troops broke and fell back. At the same time the 1st Minnesota took up positions along Plum Run. Wilcox later recalled that the Minnesota troops charged three times with bayonets.

The 1st Minnesota paid a terrible price in losses, but their commander, William Colvill new the situation was dire. The 111th New York began to back up the Minnesota troops and between that and artillery support, the Alabama troops began to take serious losses. As other Union troops began to advance, General Wilcox ordered his troop to retreat and reorganize along the Emmitsburg Road.

When this fight was over, of the 265 men of the 1st Minnesota that began the fight, only 47 remained, the rest were either killed or wounded.

I reached my selected spot for the investigation, near Plum Run at about 8:00 am in the morning. I sat down near an old oak tree that I felt might have seen the fight. The digital recorders were placed about 35 feet apart and I sat facing Plum Run but also looking toward the recorder, at a distance on the left. It was cool but pleasant and quiet, save for a few birds. The E.V.P. session lasted about 45 minutes. Recounting details of the battle, I waited for responses.

Recorder 1: Anyone know William Colvill?

Answer: "I do." (Faint)

Recorder 1: (Not associated with a question)

Answer: "I miss home." (Very faint)

Recorder 1: Wilcox's Alabama Brigade

Answer: "I'm Here." (Extremely faint)

Recorder 1: I talked of the bayonet charge.

Answer: "Ready...Ready."

Recorder 2: What do you know about this big old oak tree?

Answer: "Not Here."

Gettysburg and its rich heritage, continues to amaze the visitor, even in a remote spot, near an old oak tree, on a crisp November morning.

Chapter4

PUBLIC SPIRITS

Public spirits are those that make themselves known in places that are or were government buildings, places of entertainment, schools, streets, or even railroads. They may be witnessed over the years by generations of visitors. The stories are often well documented by this fact.

The Madison School Ghosts

James Madison School was the pride of Putnam when it was constructed in the 1850's. The school has served as a high school, a grade school, an adult education program, an early childhood program and yet today serves as a fatherhood initiative program in 2018. It has been referred to as the "Crown Jewel" in the Zanesville City School District for its long history of service to the community.

As restoration progressed in January of 1997, a strange event took place. A security system was being installed in the building and as often is the case, the work had taken longer than expected. The technician was working late hours to catch up and his work took him past midnight one evening.

His work that particular night was centered on the old basement. An eerie feeling crept over him as the steam heat kicked on. He heard the clanking, banging, and groaning as the steam passed through the pipes. He began to wonder if this night work was worth it, but the job had to get finished.

Soon the pipes went silent and peace returned to the old basement. Then, as if to taunt the man, the footsteps began. First, across the first floor above him, then, up and down the great stairway to the second floor they went. Multiple sets of footsteps could be heard.

"What is happening?" thought the technician. He feared that a group of people had broken into the building. Soon, he mastered the courage to climb the old wooden stairway up from the basement. All went suddenly quiet and he paused for a few short moments. He opened the first floor door and searched every room. There was not a window or door that wasn't locked. There was no way to enter the building and he was sure no one had left. He would have heard the heavy doors.

A student observed that she believes there are three spirits in the old building. They may be former teachers or students. Even today, many people visit the old school. They hope to capture a piece of their past, and for a moment return to the days when they were taught, worked or studied at James Madison School.

In October of 1997, during the presentation of James Madison Mourning Theatre, again an unusual event took place. As the evening's activities were coming to a close, a light apparently came on upstairs and a door opened by its self. One unbeliever began to have second thoughts.

The strange happenings at James Madison have not ceased over the years. The school, built between 1853 and 1854 may have had its first paranormal activity before the Civil War. One of the possible burial sites for the "Runaway" is the basement of this building. People for years have expressed an uneasy feeling that comes over them if they are in the basement alone. Now one may say that people sometimes feel uneasy in basements, which is true, but do consider that many of the people involved in supporting the construction of this building were also ardent abolitionists and station keepers on the Underground Railroad.

About 2003 another incident took place as James Madison School. A custodian was finishing up his evening work and was about to go home for the night. It had been a long shift and the principal's office had been his last job of the night. He sat down to relax for a moment.

As he sat there, he heard a noise downstairs. An uncomfortable feeling swept over his body and mind. Has someone broken into the building? Then, he thought about the ghost stories. He glanced at the security monitors before making a move.

A white glow seemed to be coming from one of the downstairs classrooms. The white light intensified in the room's doorway. As he stared into the monitor in disbelief, a glowing column of wispy light, in an almost human form emerged from the classroom. The light made its way into the hallway and toward the stairs and another classroom. It faded and vanished into the surrounding darkened corridor. It didn't take long for the weary worker to consider the fact that a shift change might be in order!

In 2008, members of The Ohio Paranormal Seekers team, on break from their Stone Academy investigation, made their way to the old school. Possible movement was noted in an upstairs window. A temperature gauge was pointed at the window and a large measure of temperature variation was noted there, compared to other windows. No one, among the living, was known to be present in the old historic school. The team members felt there could also be a connection between James Madison School and the Stone Academy.

Participants in our *Putnam Ghost Walks* have also made observations. Once participants reported seeing what they believed was a candle in one of the upstairs windows. Others have reported faint images in the windows and photographed some orbs as well. One participant even felt she saw two ghostly children standing by the front door. It appears that school may always be in session at James Madison School. So much of that energy comes from within the grand old building's walls, reminding us of school days past.

Visit to an Unbeliever

It is probably the most natural thing in this world to be skeptical when it comes to the subject of ghosts. What happens when our world bumps into another? Even an unbeliever must pause to question the result.

Working alone in an historic structure can have its rewards. Think what can be accomplished when there is little or no distraction? Sometimes even the most focused worker must stop to tend to the unexpected visitor.

The Stone Academy, built in 1809, is located in the Putnam Historical District of Zanesville. It is one of the most historic buildings in Ohio. In fact, it is the last government building of its time in Ohio. Today it serves as one of two museums for Muskingum History; The Pioneer and Historical Society of Muskingum County. The building served as a court, a school, a church and a meeting house in its early years. It was the site of two state abolition conferences, in 1835 and 1839. For much of its later history it was a private residence. The actress, writer, and a leader of the Women's Movement in Great Britain, Elizabeth "Bessie" Robins grew up in the historic structure. Her grandmother and father worked hard to raise her. She was one of her father's many dreams that didn't work out as he'd planned. Against his objections, she became an actress.

A devoted worker was laboring alone at the Stone Academy. She worked in the kitchen, her mind far away from thoughts of ghosts or hauntings. After all, she didn't believe in them. In the corner of her eye, she caught a movement that drew her attention away from her task.

There, in the adjoining dining area, was the figure of a man. He looked to be in his forties, tall and somewhat thin, with an angular face and long, somewhat unkempt black hair. He was wearing black pants and a long black greatcoat.

As she watched and wondered what to do next, the man made his way across the dining room, down the hallway and into what today is a cloakroom. She cautiously followed him, resolving to inquire what his business was at the house. He had looked somewhat worried to her.

She stepped into the hallway, then turned and stood at the entrance of the cloakroom. To her shock and surprise, the man was not there. He had vanished and there was no place to go. A strange sense of curiosity and fear went through her being. The room had once been near an entrance and stairway. Her visitor must have used the old floor plan, one that no living person of the present age could ever have used!

Is this ghostly visitor Elizabeth Robins' father, Charles? Had another of his dreams failed to materialize? Was it his banking career, gold prospecting, or his daughter's insistence on an acting career that causes him to continue to worry?

Could it be the great, emotional, abolitionist speaker Theodore Weld? The description seems to match him when he visited the Stone Academy in 1835. Could it be another occupant? The house had so many.

In October of 1997, an incident occurred that might in its own way support Charles Robins. It occurred in the upstairs, near where the old stairway once was.

A young woman of nineteen and her male friend of many years were exploring the old house with a flashlight. The old floorboards creaked as they made their way from the 1809 structure to the early frame addition. They paused to listen and the boards behind them continued to creak, as if trodden on by unseen feet.

The sound stopped just behind the nervous couple. The young woman fled the upstairs, followed by her friend. Upon reaching safer lit ground of the downstairs, she reported that she had felt an overwhelming presence behind her, as if someone was standing almost against her and peering over her shoulder.

The woman bears a striking resemblance to the young actress, Elizabeth Robins. She has the same captivating blue eyes and a similar build. It so happens that very night in the Stone Academy, she was one of three young women engaged in the business of acting!

It is important to note that the young woman knew little of Elizabeth Robins and that Elizabeth Robins had her own ghost in the house. She called him Yaffti Makafti and he lived under the front stairway!

Since the printing of *Ghosts in the Valley* (1998) there have been additional examples of unexplained happenings at the Stone Academy. One such incident occurred in the office area, above the garage, in the "new edition" that might date to around 1910 or 1920, possibly a little older. It happened to one of our directors.

A director was working alone in his office and archives room. Nothing was going on, no presence felt, as had been the case in a least one previous instance. It was quiet, very quiet. From somewhere behind him, the director heard his name. It was so clear. Undaunted, the director went to check if anyone was in the building. He found no one and the building was secure.

The director returned to his work. Again there it was. Someone was calling out his first name. That was it! He left the building and headed for visible, human company at the second museum. He related his story and we have it today. It is just another part of the rich, ghostly heritage of a grand old building. The adventure continues.

In 2008, we as a board, decided to allow ghost investigations at the Stone Academy. Two groups came to visit our museum, T.O.P. S. and S.E.O.P.I. Melissa and I were present and participated in the investigations. I was expected to be there as it had been my idea to allow the investigations. Both groups were skilled and took their work seriously. Missy and I joined the latter group in 2009.

Each group focused on E.V.P. (Electronic Voice Phenomena) and asked questions in the hopes of getting responses, and each was successful. I carried one recorder with me and placed another in a location and left it. In each investigation I gathered E.V.P.s.

Toward the end of the S.E.O.P.I. investigation, we were gathered in the director's office at one point. I had recalled the previous incident and one of the group's members felt a presence was in the director's room. No sooner had this been mentioned when a concentration of cold air brushed past us and into the hallway.

Later, some of us were gathered near the cloakroom, about 4:00am. This location was also near the trapdoor leading to the crawl space and a possible hiding place during the days of the Underground Railroad. We were discussing the night's events and looking at some photographs. We tried one last short E.V.P. session.

When the recorders were reviewed, an E.V.P. of a most unusual nature was captured. On my recorder I heard "Set" a click (like wooden drumsticks) and then the rat-a-tat-tat of a snare drum. The group's recorder had basically the same thing, except possibly the word "stand by" as well.

Since 2008, other groups have visited the Stone Academy and I have not known any to go away disappointed. The building literally always has something going on!

In 2016, we presented another historical program, using a ghost theme. As we told dramatic, first person stories to the crowd, Ashley Dingey and I also filmed and used E.M.F. detectors and digital recorders during the program. I played Theodore Weld, Amy Underwood played Angelina Grimke Weld and Kristen Leigh Brown read a part as Elizabeth Robins as well as played the mother of a girl whose body was stolen from Putnam Burying Ground.

As I introduced the program, and told the crowd about the ghost investigation and what one might experience, the lights blinked off and on which certainly set the mood! When the character of Elizabeth Robins was introduced, I mentioned she was an actress, a writer and worked for rights for women, we got a response from a distant female voice, on our recorder. "That's me." Apparently "Bessie", as her friends called her, was also there for our performance that night.

In October of 2017 we offered ghost walks in Putnam and the chance for an investigation at the Stone Academy. The events were well attended and during our public investigation at the Stone Academy we made contact with yet another "resident" of the place. Jonathan Hobby, who ran a school there in the early 1800's, made his presence known in a couple of E.V.P.s. Life lives on at the Stone Academy, only waiting to reveal itself to the next visitor. Hope to see you there.

The Ellis Dam Railroad Bridge

Ellis Dam is the northernmost dam on the Muskingum River. It was designed to allow boats to navigate the river up to the Dresden area. In the early days a canal system connected into the river at Dresden allowing travel by water to the Great Lakes and beyond. Just below the dam is an impressive old railroad bridge. Though it is no longer used for the railroad, it is being preserved for a bicycle path (1998).

The area has long been popular with fisherman. Our story comes to us from a man who is very familiar with the area. He has fished it for many years.

In the spring of 1913 a great flood struck the Muskingum Valley and much of Ohio. The railroad bridge at Ellis Dam was among its many victims. Only the westernmost span of the structure survived the great flood.

Even before much of the water receded, railroad crews began the job of constructing the new span of the bridge. There was a great need to keep the trains running. The work was hurried along, deadlines had been set.

On May 1, 1913, at 2:15 pm in the afternoon the trestle bent and the derrick-crane plunged into the river. After a close inspection, no attempt was made to salvage it. The trestles and pier restoration had to be inspected for work to proceed. This delayed the completion of the temporary repairs for the better part of two weeks.

Today, if one visits the bridge at night, it is reported that lights appear on the river below the bridge. They move about as if someone is searching for something, or inspecting the old bridge. The lights are not those of the small boats or fisherman, or any apparent living being. They seem to move about and sometimes appear just under the surface of the water. Then, they vanish almost as fast as they appear.

Are the workman of 1913 still inspecting the lost crane or witnesses observing some other more tragic event, lost in the pages of time? Maybe the lights are associated with a lost communal village, brick making, or the coal industry that once flourished near this location. The old river won't tell; a mystery remains to this day.

The Prison Ghost

An old prison stands by itself on a dark country road. It is located back from the road, toward the woods. When it gets dark, a fog has been known to settle in and a chill fills the air.

Late one evening near Roseville, Ohio, two young girls decided to take a walk. They came upon the old prison and decided to explore it. They walked through the door of the old prison and it was cold and dark. The girls could see the cell doors were standing open. The moonlight was glaring through a few broken windows and this served to light the inside.

Cautiously, the explorers went forward. They made their way through the old prison. The floor was wet from a leak in the roof and the air was musty. Finally, they found themselves on the roof.

There, they saw something they never would forget. The spirit of adventure was fading fast as their eyes scanned the roof and saw it. There on the other side, not far from them was, glowing in the moonlight, the white figure of a person. They were not alone.

As the girls approached, moving closer, little by little, the glowing white figure paused a moment then jumped over the side of the tall building. When the astonished girls reached the far side of the building, they stopped, gazing over the edge. They were afraid what might be on the ground below them. To their surprise, the figure had vanished. The adventurers were scared, really terrified, and ran through the dimly lit prison and all the way home. Their minds filled with unanswered questions.

Was their experience an encounter with a ghost or spirit? Perhaps they had just experienced the final scene in the life of a lonely, desperate prisoner. The girls did not return to the old forlorn prison again. Today the property is vacant and reported to be for sale (1998).

The incident that was observed by the girls has been reported by numerous individuals over the years and has almost become a legend associated with the prison. There is some debate as to who the "jumper" is, and even if it is male or female.

A second ghost has been added to the mix in recent years. This is said to be that of a prison guard who continues to maintain his post in the crumbling guard tower. As of this writing, the ownership of the old prison has changed hands, no more incidents have been reported, and no one is permitted to be on the grounds or in what remains of the prison (2009).

Fletcher Hospital

Fletcher hospital was located north of the city of Cambridge, Ohio. It was a community of buildings, constructed with brick and connected by long enclosed hallways, enabling the patients and staff to move from building to building without going outside for the most part.

The hospital was constructed during World War 2 to serve wounded and disabled soldiers returning from the war. Some German prisoners were housed there as well and they helped maintain the grounds and buildings. The hospital had a theatre, a gym, a church and other buildings which made it essentially a small community. During the war and shortly thereafter, U.S.O. shows would even visit the site. In 1946 the hospital began to transition to Cambridge State Hospital. This hospital served patients with mental health and developmental issues.

As you can imagine, many unusual incidents and some tragic deaths were a part of the long history of the hospital. There are many possibilities to consider as to reasons for hauntings but most people didn't focus too much on them. There was more concern for the living and their struggles.

One haunting seemed to be consistent over time and aspects of it were noted by individuals working in activities and education in what was called the Red Cross Building. This building was essentially a gym/ activity area with numerous additional rooms scattered over two floors. By his actions, the ghost seemed to be someone who took care of the building. Once someone felt they heard someone speaking German, so the ghost was named Hans!

Hans was often noted at night, sometimes after events at the Red Cross Building. If you were alone in the building after the patients and staff had left, or in some cases working there by yourself, you might experience "Hans".

Sometimes, fairly often, one might hear footsteps in the building or on the stairs. If the listener got up to check on who might be in the building, no one would be found. Sometimes a light might come on or returning to the building after it was closed, a light might be on that was turned off the night before. You might hear water running or a toilet flush and again find no one around the area. Some individuals would also report the feeling of a presence with them as they worked and others preferred simply to not being in the area by themselves at night.

No one ever reported seeing "Hans" but the incidents certainly pointed to some form of paranormal activity in the big, old building. It may be that the spirit was that of a person who so loved the place that they never left. So many hauntings seem to have that kind of connection.

Today, little remains of Fletcher Hospital. The Red Cross Building and nearly all the other buildings are gone. A few of the newer buildings remain and continue to be used as treatment centers and housing for patients. To my knowledge, only one corridor remains and by now it could be gone, but one question remains. Where do the spirits go? Do they still live in a world of their memories, unseen by the modern visitor? Often there are more questions than answers.

The Headless Wanderer of the Woods

Near Londonderry in Guernsey County, is a haunting that has occurred for many years. It was recorded in Wolf's *Stories of Guernsey County*. An incident from the early 1800's may explain the haunting.

Before the age of the steamboat, men often took their cargo to New Orleans for the better prices of the market there. They would sell the cargo and the boat lumber and return north on foot or horseback. They used the Natchez Trail, the Wilderness Trail, Zane's Trace and the Carpenter's Trail or old Mingo Trail to return to Pittsburgh. Robbery was a constant threat.

One day, a riderless horse, complete with bridle and saddle and saddle bags, was found along the Carpenter's Trail, today old Steubenville Road. The saddle bags were cut open and there was the sign of a struggle nearby. No rider, however, was found.

The people in the area expected foul play. Their feelings were confirmed shortly thereafter, when the reports started coming in.

Numerous residents began to report the sighting of a man wandering aimlessly around the forest. He appeared to be searching for something. Upon close examination of the stranger, it was found that the figure had no head. No body was ever found but the sightings continued long after the event. Some settlers became convinced that there might be a lost treasure and began to dig in the area. Nothing was ever reported found. Does this tortured spirit still haunt the woods about Londonderry?

Theatre Apparitions

It seems that local theatres have more than their share of ghosts and hauntings. Ghosts have been reported at Secrest Auditorium and the Opera House in McConnelsville. Unseen forces have also been said to interfere with audio-visual equipment at Ohio University, Zanesville. Marietta has them too!

Workers at Secrest Auditorium over the years have reported the shadowy figure of a man in the balcony area and have learned to live with the presence. The Opera House Ghost is described in similar terms, and is said to roam about that historic structure.

Someone once said that, "The World's a Stage!" Maybe that thought holds true on the other side as well.

Chad Hughes of the T.O.P.S. group shared with me an E.V.P. from the Secrest Auditorium in Zanesville, Ohio. It has stayed with him and just about everyone who has heard it. Chad asks, "What's it like on the other side?" The answer he gets is, "Like a Dream!"

The question that comes to mind concerning ghosts in the theatre is simply "Why?" The answer may be found in the level of emotion at such a venue or possibly have something to do with all the audio-visual equipment that is often in use there.

Paranormal investigators always complain about batteries going down and sometimes cameras malfunctioning. But then again, people who feel they have experienced the ghost at Secrest Auditorium will tell you that he seems to appear to be seated, as if watching the performance.

Late Night Fright Site

One story that has persisted over time in downtown Zanesville is that of a ghostly couple seen on Main Street. The details are few and speculation abounds.

Near the Muskingum County Courthouse on Main Street is said to be the abode of a ghostly couple. They have been reported late at night, making their way from the courthouse to the river. Both are dressed in federal period clothing which suggests an early origin for the haunting. The route is always the same as they walk arm and arm toward the river.

The area near the Y Bridge is subject to unusual currents and rapid water when the river is high. The river has claimed many lives over its history. Dr. Isaac Fowler crashed his buggy into the deadly waters, missing the bridge in a thick fog. Ebenezer Buckingham and Jacob Boyd died when a span of the new Y Bridge collapsed when it was being built in 1837. Earlier, a companion of John McIntire and James Taylor, Peter Urie, drowned when slept over a wing dam. A boat the three were using had capsized in high water. Just upriver, on the Licking River, a whole family had been lost in high water, and buried on the river bank. There are so many possibilities, the mystery remains.

The Muskingum County Courthouse

The day when court is in session is always a busy day. Much has to be accomplished before, during and after a session is held. Emotions can be in a heightened state as the law is administered. Sometimes the energy seems to expand beyond the court that is in session.

Two courtroom areas are located side by side and can be busy at the same time. The only difference is that one is vacant! Sometimes it sounds as though someone is going through papers or documents as one can hear the rustling noise as the work continues. You might hear the sound of books placed on a table or possibly even faint footsteps. Sometimes a light goes on and off. If one goes over to check the room, it is found empty.

It seems that court is always is session in this world and on the other side.

University Ghosts

With its origins in an academy associated with the Presbyterian Church, Muskingum College was chartered on March 18, 1837. Today it has been elevated to the status of Muskingum University. It has a long history of providing outstanding education to its students. Many have gone on to become well known in their fields of study and endeavors.

Montgomery Blvd. is known to some as Professors' Row. A well known and loved art professor made the beautiful old tree lined street his own, residing there for many years. He loved to teach and often had his students over to his house in small groups. Coffee Cloches were held each year while he was teaching. Many a pleasant hour was spent in his company. The professor was getting up in years but loved Europe and looked forward to his visits there. One year, while in Italy, he passed away.

After his passing, students utilized his house as a residence. Some feel the professor continues to reside there with them today. There is a warm, loving feeling that they have experienced in his presence. Glimpses of the professor appear from time to time in a misty, transparent form. One coed reported that she was on her way to the basement and stumbled on the steps. An unseen hand supported her and prevented the fall. She was happy that Professor "Louie" as they call him was there when she needed him.

Another story that has come to light of recent is that of a haunted walking trail. The trail starts at a location near the football stadium and extends up a hollow toward the campus of John Glenn High School.

The trail passes the site of a log cabin that once stood in the hollow in the mid to late 1970's, when my brother and I attended Muskingum, and follows a small stream. In 2017 I began to hear strange stories, beyond the campus activities there; that suggest paranormal activity.

Strange sounds have been heard, orbs photographed and unusual lights have been noted. It seems an investigation and E.V.P. session might be in order.

With its long history and heritage, Muskingum University continues to provide an education worth having and sharing. Other incidents have come to attention over the years; the ghostly form of a woman in a dorm window, ghosts in the old theatre and Johnson Hall, now both demolished and of recent, the photo of what may be a ghostly form at the new memorial by the old college spring.

The Market House Tragedy

Market Street in Zanesville is named thus because in part of the large market house that stood where the city building does today. Produce was bought and sold there, from field crops to garden plots to products made from the home. On January 24, 1863, tragedy stuck.

It was a harsh winter and snow and ice had been piling up just about everywhere. The market had opened that day and was well underway. There was a loud crack as a part of the roof gave way and collapsed upon the vendors and customers. Timbers, slates, ice and snow fell among the victims. Four people were soon dead and sixteen others injured.

Sensitives will tell you they feel the pain and desperation of the victims. The haunting questions; "Where's my family?" "Are they dead or alive?" "Someone please help me!" Events like this are not soon forgotten, in this world or the next. Does the tragedy of that day somehow remain here, repeated over time? It is not unlike the video clip, played over and over, shared with those who come to it, as they scan their social media feed.

Nice River Lot - E.V.P. Available

The riverfront along Muskingum Avenue in Zanesville, Ohio was once a thriving industrial area, served by a railroad line. Gravel was dug from the river. Small industries dotted the banks including laundry operations, a glass house, a tannery and even a glove factory. Pottery was made there and later there was a postcard factory too. A riverboat landing was maintained at present day Putnam Landing Park. Scraps of the area's past sometimes wash out of the river banks after episodes of high water.

In fact, the 1913 Flood destroyed much of the industry located along Muskingum Avenue. Today most of the buildings are gone; though a few buildings, used mostly for storage, remain in the vicinity. The railroad is gone; a few foundations remain as do some access points that lead to nothing.

As one makes their way down Madison Street, you will pass a building that was once used as an early childhood and adult education center. Today it serves as a crematory. The empty field by the river was the site of an unusual incident.

In 2006 and 2007 our classes sometimes visited the area to take photographs and look for Bald Eagles that sometimes visit in winter or early spring. The students were getting excited about developing web sites where they could share their pictures and make new friends.

On one of our visits we found some rotting, discarded women's clothing, including undergarments, amongst the overgrowth of grass and brush. The students, all women, paused for a moment and joked about who might have been there and what they were up to. Soon we were taking pictures for the web sites and practicing portraits in a natural setting. No one thought any more of the old cloths.

That night as I put the pictures into the computer I noticed a sound file amongst the digital pictures, even though we had not done any sound recording. I was able to retrieve the sound file and a woman's voice apparently said, "Help Me". The jokes about the clothes of yesterday turned to consternation and wondering for some of the students the next morning! What if the ghost followed us back to school?

Our group chose to shoot the next set of pictures in our class area. The images were beautiful and everyone was happy, apparently including our newest student. As the images were once again put into the computer, a second sound file appeared! This time, no words, only a high pitched giggling! For me, sometimes E.V.P. just happens. On further study of the first E.V.P., some felt the words may have been "Hug me." We never heard any more from our newest student but some felt she stayed with our class.

The Increase Mathews House

The Increase Mathews House, built in 1805 from stone quarried on Putnam Hill is the oldest structure in Zanesville and is one of two museums run by our Muskingum History group. It has hosted school tours for many years and the visitor gets to experience different aspects of our history. History comes alive there.

A number of years ago a school tour was visiting the house, and the group of students seemed very interested in the museum, save one. This little boy was always getting into mischief. Sometimes he would torment the other children and even make some cry.

This "tough" guy decided to give the group "the slip." He ducked into an upstairs room and hid behind a door. The group didn't see him and continued on the tour. "What fun is this?" he thought. No one was looking for him and it was getting awfully quiet. The floor creaked a little on the other side of the door.

As he stepped out from behind the door, he quickly saw he was not alone. There directly in front of him stood an African American child, about his age. His old time ragged clothes and look said he wasn't from the world of the living. This child said nothing, but his gaze did not look away from the mischief maker. As the student fled into the hall, the ghostly child vanished. The mischief maker ran crying to his teacher that he has seen a ghost! That day the other students got a laugh at the boy's expense.

Other things happen in the old house, and it seems to happen when someone is there working alone. Unusual creaks and sounds are heard, maybe even footsteps, but then again, it's an old house. Then, maybe there is a rustling in the old doctor's office, someone sifting through papers. A presence is felt. There certainly is more to an old house than always meets the eye.

Keep your eyes open, keep your digital recorders running, and don't hide from your friends. The Increase Mathews House is a great place to visit.

The P.U.R.E. Center

The Putnam Underground Railroad Center was located on Woodlawn Avenue. It was built by Francis Potts, a Putnam business man before the Civil War. Mr. Potts had two sons in the war and his daughter taught at the Putnam Female Seminary. It served until recently as a museum and education area. Today the collection is housed at different locations throughout Zanesville.

After the Potts family no longer lived there, it became an apartment house until it was restored for use as the P.U.R.E. Center. During its time as an apartment complex an unusual event occurred.

A former student remembered a strange incident that occurred late one night. She was awakened by a strange sound in the hallway. Strange noises were heard upstairs. She opened the door of her apartment to see a glowing white light that moved across the floor. As she watched, the light faded and vanished. She has always wondered just what she saw, or possibly who.

Photographs

The Old Quaker Burying Ground, Site of the Grave of Moses Dillon, p.4

(Gary Felumlee, 2018)

Norwich Presbyterian Cemetery, p.7

(Gary Felumlee, 2018)

Stumpy Hollow, Near Norwich, Ohio p.8

(Gary Felumlee, 2018)

Spirit 7 Members Investigating at Gettysburg Pa.

Left to Right: Keith, Gary and Aaron Felumlee (Melissa Felumlee, 2011)

"There's Ectoplasm on the Bridge."p.35

Melissa was humming Civil War music and dancing as white columns seemed to be forming around her. Sach's Bridge; Gettysburg, Pa. (Gary Felumlee, 1999)

Waiting for Jeremy, Farnsworth House; Gettysburg Pa. p.39 (G.Felumlee,2009)

Chapter 5

FAMILY TIES

Sometimes hauntings seem to be the result of close emotional bonds in a family. This can be for good or bad. The following stories are those of ghosts with family ties.

Prospect Place

At Trinway, just north of Dresden in Muskingum County sits a stately old abandoned mansion that was built prior to the Civil War. (1998 edition) Today this mansion is anything but abandoned, as it is now known as the George W. Adams Education Center and is the site of historical tours and educational activity. It is also known for its paranormal activity and has been the subject of television episodes, as well as public and private paranormal investigations.

George W. Adams had had the mansion built in 1856 for his second wife and his family. Prospect Place was a reflection on Adams' achievements as a merchant and community builder. As it was being completed, it was burnt. Arson was labeled the cause and the reason apparently was that one of the workers wanted to continue his job as a builder! Prospect Place was soon rebuilt and due to Mr. Adams strong abolition sentiments, served as a station on the Underground Railroad, along with being his family residence.

A mother and daughter were living at Prospect Place at the time of the American Civil War. The winter had turned bitterly cold and many suffered as a result of the weather.

The mother loved her child very much and didn't know what she would ever do without her. Love just wasn't enough that cold winter and the child sickened and died. The mother was heartbroken and mourned her little child.

The freezing temperatures of this bitter winter had frozen the ground to a great depth. It would be impossible to dig her grave until the spring thaw. The poor unfortunate little one was given a temporary resting place in a cool room in the basement of the mansion.

Her mother, filled with grief and sorrow, visited the dead child every day, sometimes several times a day. She would sit with her daughter and think of the songs she used to sing and the stories she used to tell. The emotional toll was terrible. The mother could not seem to let go. In the spring, the child was buried.

The years passed by, the families in the old mansion changed and the mother joined her child in death. The child, however, never left the old house. She apparently is unable or unwilling to leave the place where she found so much love.

Her shadowy form is said to appear near one of the fireplaces in the mansion. A visitor to the house caught her faint image on film. She was taking a group shot and the faint image of a young girl appeared behind the group.

Perhaps more frightening is the experience of a girl who lived across the road from Prospect Place. She awakened to see the glowing image of a young girl at the foot of her bed. The ghostly girl looked longingly at her living counterpart. Perhaps she longed to trade places and live the life that death denied her.

This story is the story that encouraged Melissa and I to investigate Prospect Place in 1992. It was our first investigation and we used only a camera, in hopes of getting a picture. We had heard the Adams Mansion was to be torn down and got permission to visit.

The house was in a terrible state, mantles were stolen or broken, fireplace tile was scattered about, the stairway was damaged and the ball room had graffiti, and there was wax from candles around a pentagram on the floor. We thought at the time that this would likely be our last visit to this once stately structure that time and vandals had treated so badly.

We could not find research to support the story of the little girl but thought that the child may have been associated with someone who worked there, possibly a servant. A second story associated with the Mansion was of a photograph of two young boys, one wearing a coonskin cap, who appeared in another individual's picture. We thought of the two Adams brothers as children growing up in the vicinity of Prospect Place or the surrounding area.

After several pictures, and time exploring, we left the mansion. We had some interesting pictures but no picture of a little girl or the two boys. One picture was interesting, showing sunlight coming through window slates and forming a bright orb-like image and another that just seemed to be a bad shot, maybe I moved too much!

Years later I was going through some pictures and came across the images once again. My "goofed" image came up and turned out to be our most ghostly one. We saw across the ballroom from Missy the image of a young woman with long hair. She wasn't our little girl but there is certainly the possibility that her spirit form was that of a younger woman, a family member, who did indeed pass in the house. Ghosts do linger, even on photographs!

Aaron Chandler, a member of our Spirit 7 group, now resides in Georgia. For a number of years he served as a tour guide and artist for Prospect Place. He painted portraits of some of the family members and would often carry around a digital recorder as he went about the house. He was there for many paranormal investigations.

One strategy he liked to use for recording E.V.P.'s was to leave a digital recorder in a room after a tour went through. He was often rewarded for his efforts by short statements from the ghostly inhabitants. Sometimes, he would drop in, greet the spirit world; maybe even bring something to the room. One of the younger ladies was recorded to exclaim, "Aaron," in a sweet, loving way! Kindness appears to be universal, in this world and the next.

So many individuals and groups have investigated and explored Prospect Place since the publication of *Ghosts in the Valley* in 1998. Most are impressed with the wonderful history of the old mansion and its occupants. There is so much to learn and experience.

Participants in the paranormal investigations, have over the years, made contact through E.V.P.s (Electronic Voice Phenomena) with many individuals apparently associated with the house. Recordings have been made of older and younger adult voices, children, and even possible travelers on the Underground Railroad.

The mansion has a web site, The George W. Adams Education Center and a Facebook page. Your support is greatly appreciated as the director, Jeff Cole and his Board of Trustees, continue to work to maintain and restore Prospect Place for the future.

The Baby's Cries

Sometimes, even the strongest bonds, those between a mother and her baby, can go wrong. Then, maybe it would have been better if the child was not born at all. So was the case for a mother and her baby that lived all alone, on a side street, which once extended up Putnam Hill from Woodlawn Avenue in Zanesville.

Shortly after the child's birth, the father had abandoned his family. The mother set about the task of raising her child, knowing that she would certainly face hardships as the child grew up. At first, all went well. The infant and mother began life together. The little baby slept most of the time and the mother went about her routine. Then the crying started.

Some nights the baby would cry and cry and no matter what the mother did, the crying continued. Night after night the crying continued. The mother would feed the little one, hold it and sing to it, but the crying continued. Sometimes it seemed the more the mother did, the louder the crying got.

One late night, the mother, unable to take the crying, finally snapped. She grabbed that crying baby and shook it. The crying continued until the mother's grasping, desperate hands strangled the baby.

She took the still quivering body and cut it to pieces. She cut off the arms, legs and head, placing the mutilated body in a bag, in her cabinet. Later she was said to transfer this to her trash that was carried away to the dump. The deed was done and the murderess had escaped, disappearing from the area.

The next family to live in the house began to hear the sound of a crying baby. Some nights the sound seemed to carry throughout the house. The search always came up empty and the crying would stop before its source was discovered.

One night, the family was up later than usual. As they sat around the living room, the crying started. It seemed to be coming from the kitchen. They made their way to the kitchen and stood before a cabinet. The cries seemed to come from inside.

They threw open the cabinet door and there, to their horror, was the glowing, deteriorating, floating head of an infant. Tears streamed down its face and its mouth moved as its cries filled the room. The cries ceased and the image disappeared.

Philo Bridge

Duncan Falls and Philo sit across from each other on the Muskingum River. Located at a site that once included a set of rapids, often referred to as Duncan's Falls that provided water power for early industry. The towns today are connected by an old, narrow bridge though a new one is to be built, in 2018. Some years ago a tragedy took place that may in part reoccur today, according to local tradition.

An older child had been left with the responsibility of caring for the family infant. He had had other plans and sorely missed his friends. He thought he had the problem solved. He would take the baby and still go out with his friends. The plan was to be back before he was missed.

The teenagers were soon concerned with other things, disregarding the baby in their care. The night was young and there were girls to see and other activities to do.

They were showing off the car, maybe driving too fast, when they missed the bridge and plunged into the river. It was a bad accident, the baby was not found until sometime later, its life snuffed out as fast as if someone had blown out a candle.

It is said that sometimes after dark, if you go down to the bridge on the Philo side, that the baby's cries may still be heard. Sometimes a lack of responsibility has tragic consequences.

Grandparents to the Rescue

Many have fond memories of their close relationships with their grandparents. You could always count on a grandparent to come through in times of need. Sometimes a hug, a piece of candy or a smile made things right.

Grandparents help to keep us out of trouble and are always concerned about our safety. Their concern has continued, some say, into the world beyond that of the living. They have interceded to prevent catastrophe.

Two incidents that occurred in the Muskingum Valley are presented here. Both saved an infant or toddler from harm.

In the first, a young mother had brought her baby home to see her parents. She was saddened as her grandfather had recently died and not lived to see the baby after its birth. The tired mother took a moment to rest with her baby on the couch.

She was alone in the room and thinking of her grandfather. The next incident she felt the infant fall from her grasp! Her heart leaped to her throat as she waited to hear the baby hit the floor. The baby never did and the next thing she knew, she felt a pair of strong arms return the baby to her grasp. There was the smell of familiar pipe smoke, and she knew who her rescuer was. Her grandfather had saved her child.

Greasy Grandma was what the other bikers called their companion. It was a sad day when she passed away. She was always remembered with affection by her friends.

Sometime later the club had gotten together for a cookout. It was a time for friends to share old memories and renew the bonds of friendship.

One child had strayed from his parents' sight. The toddler had made his way to the top of a second story deck, and at the last moment the adults noticed him. It was too late.

The child plunged headfirst from the deck. In midair, he seemed to change position as if someone was holding him. He hit the ground gently as if someone had sat him there. "Greasy Grandma caught me," he said to his amazed parents.

Keeping Track of the Family

When a family pulls up roots and moves, what happens to those who are left behind? Do ghosts favor familiar surroundings or are they attached to personal items or people?

An elderly lady lived with her daughter, son-in-law and granddaughter. In her later years she often stayed in her upstairs bedroom as stairs were a problem for her. She enjoyed her television and reading. Ghost stories and mysteries were the "bill of fare" as often as not. She had many visitors and enjoyed most of the company.

One evening, she was engrossed in a book, when a visitor came calling. She heard the footsteps on the stairs, slow and deliberate. Then, the boards creaked in the hall. The family had all retired to bed long ago, so who could this be?

She believed the house next door on Oakland Boulevard in Cambridge was haunted, but now there seemed to be a presence just outside in the hall.

Her eyes strained to see the visitor, but nothing was there. Though frightened, curiosity got the best of her. She continued to listen and watch as she pulled the blankets up a little tighter.

Then, a dark shadow seemed to appear in the hall. It appeared to be a man in an old fashioned dark suit. Though the image was less than clear, she thought of her own father. As she did, the image vanished, never again to be visible.

A bit shaken from her encounter, she soon recovered and returned to her reading. You see, this was not her first experience. As a child in Cleveland, she had once been visited by a woman in dark clothes. Though frightened by the incident, she described the woman, and saw an old photograph. The woman had been her aunt; an aunt who had died before she was born.

Later, there was an old family rocker that rocked by itself, and if one listened closely, the pages of a newspaper were heard to rustle. The spirit world had always followed her about; the dark visitor was nothing unusual.

Still Searching the Family House

An unusual haunting is said to occur on Grandview Avenue in Zanesville. It was first reported by the house's newest owners in 1997.

The house was built and owned by the same family from the 1920's through most of the 1980's. Since the early 1970's an older lady had lived there. She loved her cats, children and bowling and had traveled a good bit after the passing of her husband, who had been a railroad agent most of his life.

Things went well until in the early 1980's she was the victim of a series of break-ins. In the worst incident, she was sprayed with mace and most of her jewelry was stolen. She remained in the house a few more years but health issues caused her to move to the Helen Purcell Home. She continued her bowling until 1987, when at the age of 87 she received a bowling trophy. She passed away in 1991.

Today it is said that footsteps are heard climbing the stairs and sounds come from her old bedroom. The sound most noted is that of dresser drawers opening and the jingling of jewelry. It sounds as though someone is searching the dresser drawers. Does she still hope to find some family heirloom that is missing or is she just getting ready for another trip or maybe a night of bowling? Some spirits seem to be emotionally attached to places where they spent much of their lives. We see that over and over again in our investigations.

No need to investigate this one further, my brother and I sometimes sat on the porch roof to watch fireworks launched from Putnam Hill Park. You see, this was our grandmother's house all those years ago.

Ghosts in the Paden House

Sometimes houses are said to be haunted but evidence is hard to find. Paden House is one of these. (1998) However, over time things can change.

Occupied by the same family from 1882 to about 1939, the spirit world might be thought to have strong connections. In fact, the prominent Muskingum College family that lived there in the old Queen Anne style house with double bay windows certainly left their mark on local history. The father had come from Pennsylvania and had a farm and orchard, but at one point he also served the town as marshal. One of his sons, Thomas H. Paden taught at Muskingum College for fifty years and his wife, Sadie Paden was the State Recording Secretary of the Women's Christian Temperance Union for a time.

One of the town's oldest residents (1998) today is unshakeable in her belief that the house is haunted. She does not know by whom or what but she also knows it was later used to house students and yet another family spent many years there. We purchased the house in 1989 and did some restoration there.

Some things began to happen shortly after purchase as some restoration and remodeling got under way. Once, it was late, and there was the sound of shattering glass, like someone had taken a drink and thrown the glass into the fireplace. A quick and startled check of the downstairs produced nothing. Another time, there was the sound of something or someone falling. That happened twice but again nothing was ever found.

Tradition says that during her later years Mrs. Paden had a bad fall and was laid up for some time, possibly crippled in her last year. Could this explain the noise? Professor Paden was known at one point to have broken from his church over music, as the early church used only vocal music, no organs or pianos. He had transferred to another more traditional Presbyterian Church. Could this be why things happened?

Since 1998, there has been a knocking sound, three knocks, like someone is at the door. This has happened two or three times, always at night. In each case, no earthly visitors were noted. A new event seems to confirm past suspicions.

It was October 31, 2007 and it had been a long day. Missy was feeling down, so to speak. Halloween is her favorite time of the year and she had scarcely any time to enjoy it that year, being so busy. I had come home from work and was talking up a little Halloween. "It's Beggar's Night, you know!" Her only response was, "This is just about the worst Halloween, for me, ever!"

With that there was a crash! The Halloween tray over the kitchen door fell to the floor. It was supported by a magnetic hanger that had never let loose before, nor since!

"What happened?" I exclaimed. "The Halloween tray just flew off the wall!" she answered. "Don't touch anything or move, let me get a picture!" I called back. I took two photographs in rapid succession.

The first caught the culprit. A small white ball of energy, an orb, was caught streaking from the scene of the crime! Paden House does seem to have at least one extra occupant. It was a Halloween to remember!

The Final Visit

A family once lived in Brush Creek Township in Sothern Muskingum County. Tragedy came to them one day, when they received word of the death of their son/brother at the age of 26. He was a truck driver and there had been an accident. The funeral had been held and with difficulty, the family accepted their personal loss.

About two months after the accident, the young man's older sister was awakened from her sleep. She opened her tired eyes, to see standing at the foot of her bed her lost brother.

At first she was very frightened, but then her brother smiled at her and all fear left her. He turned from her bed and walked from her room. Never again did he appear before her but somehow there was an inner peace that came to her. To this day, that peace is there when she thinks of him.

Grandma's Farm

The neighbor had called and called, but there was no answer. A quick visit to the old farmhouse told the grim tale. Grandma was there, but lying crosswise over her bed, her hand on her heart but the victim of an aneurysm. She had died.

The family gathered at her house the day of the funeral. They began the sad task of going through the fragments of her life that she left behind. Progress was slow but if everyone helped, the job would be easier.

One of her sons began to go through the things in her bedroom. He felt uneasy. As he worked, he happened to catch a glimpse of the bed through the corner of his eye. To his sheer horror, there was the image of his mother on the bed in the exact same position the neighbor had found her. He fled the room pale and shaken. "What's wrong?" asked his nephew. He recounted the story to the shocked family.

Work resumed and the nephew heard a stirring in the kitchen. He asked if someone had taken Grandma's cat. He was assured that the cat was not there. He made his way to the kitchen.

As he entered the kitchen, he observed the figure of his grandmother, bent over and working by the stove. She stood up straight and turned to face her grandson. As he watched, speechless, she turned from him and walked from the kitchen to the barn. That was the last time he saw his grandmother and he will never forget it.

Punishment from Beyond the Grave

In this second story from near East Fultonham, in Muskingum County, the memory of the grandparents is not so pleasant. A grandmother remembered being harshly punished by her parents for mistakes she had made. Even after their deaths, upon making a mistake, she seemed to see their faces and hands as they struck at her. With each error she made, her face would flinch as if it was receiving a blow from unseen hands.

She left her grandson a glass rabbit, and vowed never to strike him. To her, the glass rabbit was fragile and delicate and needed to be well treated. It would be a symbol to him of how a person should be treated. Sometimes the pains of childhood scar the adult.

Grandma's Rose

There is a small farm on Coopermill Road, just west of Zanesville, Ohio. It has been in the same family for over thirty years. There are two houses on the place, a small one near the road and the old house, grandma's house, back the lane and over a small bridge. Doug's grandma had lived in the old house while Doug and his wife Anita lived near the road. Doug's grandmother loved her flowers and kept a beautiful garden of them until the time came that she could no longer care for herself or them. After she left, the place began to decline. Grandma died and her garden with her.

Carol moved into the old house in late 2001. She knew Doug and Anita and this is her story.

I moved to the old house in 2001. In the spring I would work outside planting flowers. Anita would come up for coffee and tell me stories of Doug's grandmother. She had known her for a number of years.

One day Anita comes over and she tells me that she lived in the house after grandma's death. At times she would feel that someone was around or going up and down the steps. Sometimes the sound of a car coming up the drive would alert her that visitors were coming. Looking outside, no car was visible.

Once Doug and Anita came over to tell me how nice the yard looked and just how much grandma loved her flowers. He said she had flowers everywhere and he hated to mow there. He always "caught it" if he cut any flowers down by mistake.

I worked hard on my flowerbeds and the next year when I was out working on them I noticed a rose bush coming up in front. I asked Doug about it. He said it was his grandmother's bush. She had planted them all over the place. Anita and Doug thought it strange to see grandma's rose bush return to her garden after so many years. From their porch, they could look up at the house. It was like grandma was there.

I moved from the old place in 2006. Until then, I always planted spring flowers and perennials. Some of my favorites were Lilies of the Valley, Black Eyed Susans and Tulips. Grandma's roses began to bloom too.

Housekeepers for Eternity

There is a small one and a half story house located on Pine Street near St. Luke's Lutheran Church in Zanesville. It is the site of an interesting and responsive haunting. One might say it is a very active place and has been so since the 1940's. One couple seems to have "stayed on" since that time.

The neighborhood, when it was built was family oriented and mostly occupied by individuals who had spent careers in manufacturing and business. It wasn't a wealthy neighborhood but was a nice place to grow up and to live a comfortable life. It was a place to get attached to; a place one might not want to leave.

An older couple had built there, perhaps spending much of their savings on a new house in a new neighborhood. There was room for a charming little garden and lots of friendly neighbors. Time passes and eventually the old couple with it. Their time there was but a fading memory to only a small number of elderly neighbors.

Fifty years pass and new families come and go but life goes on, in this case, hand in hand with the afterlife. Two recent families can certainly attest to that. The first, shortly before moving began to hear things, noises at first. They were hard to explain but could be dismissed with a rational explanation. The house settled. The noise came from outside. A vibration from a passing truck caused the rattling. Then there was the fleeting image of an older man in 1940's attire, down to the coat and hat. The rational explanations were now as fleeting as the image; that seemed to reoccur.

Neighbors talk and now a new set of owners hear the story and the noises begin. One night the new couple hears a rustling and rattling. It is loud enough to demand an investigation. Slowly and quietly the couple creeps toward the source of the disturbance, only to find absolutely nothing. They remember being told of the old couple and that the woman's name may have been Margaret.

The next time something occurs it is late at night and the lady of the house is alone. Her husband has had to work the late shift again. The noise is disturbing and the fact there is no visible source of it, even more upsetting. It was a time for action.

Looking in the direction of the noise, and refusing to be frightened from her home, the lady exclaims, "Margaret, if you two are going to stay here, you must not make so much noise!"

From that time on, noise was never a problem for the family. Until the day they moved, the house was peaceful.

It appears that at least one little girl continued to enjoy a ghostly grandparent or two. She would look to the corner of the room and just laugh. On one occasion she was asked who she was looking at. She turned and smiled but on looking back to the corner, her performer had disappeared. Her face went from laughing to a little sad, her friend had gone.

A new family moved into the residence but in a short time left. There was a brief visit to the house by the prior family. The wife knew the realtor who was showing the old home and dropped in to see the place. She noticed the changes that had taken place and as she went to leave, the door mysteriously jammed. It took some time to work it open.

It appears that the "old folks at home" wanted their old family back. To this day, the lady often wonders what is going on at her old home on Pine Street.

Margaret and her husband may still reside at the old home place. If so, they appear to listen to their living counterparts. Is anyone listening to you right now? What was that noise? I'm sure there is a rational explanation.

Ashley's Dog

Do ghosts haunt our dreams? A long time ago a friend told me that they do. I thought it was pretty stupid. In one weird night, all that changed for me.

It was Thanksgiving Day in 2002 and as usual my brother went out to feed our dogs. He found two of our dogs were not moving. They had both died during the night. He ran over to me yelling, "Ash, they are both dead." I ran over to them to double check and it was true.

I hung my head and started to cry while my brother walked into the house to get dad. In a few minutes, both dogs were buried. Later that night my brother and I went to bed. That was when something very weird happened.

I dreamed I was walking down a dark tunnel and out of nowhere I saw my dog, "Little Dude," right there in front of me. I got on my knees and cried. I played with him, I talked to him and I was having so much fun. Somehow I realized this would never happen again.

Just before I woke from the dream, "Little Dude" spoke to me. He said, "Always believe in yourself!" I woke with a start and ran to my brother's room.

"Did you see our dog's ghost in your dream?" I said.

His answer was startling, "Yeah, I think so but I don't believe in ghosts anyway, Ash."

I went out to my dogs' graves and there I made a promise to them. I promised to always believe in myself and never give up. For a number of years after that night I always wore his license tag around my neck. It was there to remind me of my promise. Today, I still believe his ghost visited me that night and kept my spirits up during a very hard time.

Chapter 6

Haunted Habitats: Houses to Trailers

The most common ghost of them all is the ghost that haunts a particular dwelling place. In most cases, the ghost is that of a former occupant who will not give up his or her earthly dwelling place. Sometimes a tragic incident may prevent the spirit from leaving. In a few rare cases, it may be the location that is haunted, the modern structure being of no importance.

Indians have been reported in a Perry County basement, as has a wolf. In Muskingum County, a man dressed in Victorian clothing haunts a modern trailer. In another case, which may be pure fantasy, witches were said to haunt a fireplace in another modern trailer. All of the above examples seem out of place and, if accurate, may be location hauntings.

Usually the stories from haunted houses include doors that open for no reason, footsteps in the night and on stairways, glass breaking or activity in closed up rooms. Many abandoned homes are labeled "haunted" and hauntings are said to occur during episodes of remodeling or restoration. The following stories are interesting examples collected from the occupants themselves. Each believes their story to be true and accurate.

Abode of the Blue Lady and Her Friends

An old Steamboat Gothic house is in the Putnam section of Zanesville. The house was built by the once prominent Black family, immigrants from Ireland. They were leaders in the Republican Party in the late 1800's and early 1900's. Later the house was used as a boarding house for workers in the Putnam area.

During its history as a boarding house, the house was run by a husband and wife as well as the wife's unmarried sister. All were immigrants to this country, as were many of the workers in Putnam. Shortly after World War 1, death separated the owners from their business, possibly during the great influenza epidemic.

The husband decided to do some outdoor trimming in anticipation of spring growth. He caught pneumonia and died. Within about a week's time, both sisters took sick and died suddenly. The sisters were buried on the same day and were the first citizens of Putnam to be transported to their final resting places in a motorized hearse.

The present owners of the house (1998) have had multiple experiences which are not easy to explain. Doors are said to open on their own, and footsteps can be heard on the floors and stairway. A presence is sometimes felt in the kitchen area and sometimes at night, pots and pans clink, as do dishes and glasses, as if someone is working in the kitchen.

A visitor to the house had an experience he will never forget. Sleeping in the guest room, he awakened with an uneasy feeling. His eyes searched the room and came to rest upon the glowing, blue apparition of a stout woman in a long gown standing at the foot of his bed. Her eyes seemed to glare at him as if to say, "Get out of my room!" He was quick to oblige her and vowed to never stay in that room again.

In another incident, a man awakened to the feeling that someone had put some weight over his throat to stop his breathing. In this case, no apparition appeared but a presence seemed to be in the room. No further harm came to the man.

There have been a few electronic tricks, such as lights going on and off, but the owners love their old house and have learned to live with their ghostly occupants.

A few years after the publication of the original *Ghosts in the Valley*, incidents continued to happen in the old house. They may be related to the blue lady or another occupant of the place, a boarder.

One of the upstairs rooms seems to continue as a boarding room. This haunting may relate to a worker that was said to live there. The man was a hard worker but on Saturday he was also a hard drinker. One night he went too far, it was his last earthly night as a living being.

No one knows if he fell or jumped from his room but the next morning he was found dead on the ground below his window. He was loved as a personable man but pitied, as he was an alcoholic. His modest funeral was held and his life story ended.

His spirit remains in the place he called home, or that is what we suspect. Sometimes a chilling presence is felt. At least once his spirit reached out to the living. It was an experience the lady of the house never forgot.

It was late in the evening and she was feeling tired. She decided to rest and was soon asleep. Sometime later she awoke from a restless sleep. A freezing cold sensation began in her hand and soon spread over her body. She sensed a presence by her side, holding her hand. Was the ghost in a caring mode, watching over his living host?

She didn't know what his purpose was but she began to wear a light mitten or glove when she wanted to take a nap. She continued to live in the old house after her husband passed away and lived there until she joined him in the next world.

The Mansion Ghosts of Old Putnam

The Putnam Historic District seems to have more than its share of paranormal activity. The area was once very prosperous and a number of wealthy families called the village home. A number of large mansions were built, the last in the early 1900's. There seems to be a romantic attachment to the place, something that draws one to a place and a time that no living person remembers. Maybe that time somehow lives on, on the other side.

Two of the old mansion houses sit almost across from each other on Putnam Avenue, State Route 22. They are the Achaeur and Schultz mansions. Both are said to be haunted.

The Achaeur House was built in the early 1800's. Later in the same century it was given a more Victorian look. Recently (1998) after extensive prolonged work, the mansion was sold. Some work had to be redone and there seemed to plans for it to become a bed and breakfast.

In 1996, as the new owners worked on their project the first incident was reported to happen. One of the owners, who had told this story to a friend, emerged from an upstairs room, to see the figure of a man in a brown suit standing in the hallway.

The man had a worried expression on his face, bowed his head and clasped his hands, as if to wring them. The owner thought the man had come in from the street and confronted him. To her surprise, the figure dematerialized, as in shock of disbelief, she looked on. In an instant he was gone.

In 1997, the worried spirit again made his presence known. This time the spirit appeared in the house, looking over the bannister from the second floor to the first. It has been speculated that the ghost may be the spirit of Mr. Sturtevant, a wealthy department store owner who once made his residence in the mansion.

The Schultz Mansion is an elegant early 1900's structure, complete with gardens and a carriage house. Today it serves as a meeting place and formal dining establishment (1998). In 2018, it is being offered for sale and has been a private residence for some time and lovingly cared for.

It was once the Schultz family home. Mrs. Schultz may still be in residence, over sixty years (1998) after she crashed her Stutz Bearcat, ending her life.

Today it is reported that unusual happenings occur in her former residence. Lights are said to go on and off by themselves, toilets flush with no one in the bathroom and on one occasion, a prank was played by unseen hands.

A party was to be held at the mansion and the decorations were going up. Among the decorations were the ever popular helium filled balloons. All was ready for the event and everyone left for the night.

The next morning as the workers arrived, they found the balloons were no longer in place. They had all been moved to a new location. They now rested under the grand piano. Did Mrs. Schultz not approve of their use? Maybe it was her butler, tiding up. Some suggest he is around yet. Then again, maybe Mrs. Schultz wanted everyone to know she was still with them, at least in spirit.

In recent years, a young girl has been noted at the Achaeur House in the vicinity of the stairs and one of the Putnam Ghost Walks, before the Schultz Mansion became a private residence once again, produced the ghostly image of what appears to be a woman looking toward the street from above the main entrance and the image of a man in top hat, sitting in a second window. The physical world changes what about the realm of the spirit?

A Spirit Story

Six years ago, (1998) a young woman and her husband had just moved to their first apartment together. It was located in a house on Greenwood Avenue in Zanesville. Nothing unusual happened right away but that was to change.

The first incident happened after about a month. The wife and husband were sitting in her mother-in law's apartment, which was downstairs. They were talking about nothing important. The next thing they knew, there were footsteps coming from their apartment above. This just wasn't possible they thought. The footsteps came down the stairs toward the apartment they were now in. They paused at the door which the wife had locked. Slowly the door began to open!

As the couple sat there speechless, both their door and the adjoining door opened to where they were seated. The ghostly footsteps passed them and headed toward the basement. The noise increased as the spirit being descended the old wooden stairs to the basement.

The astonished pair followed their unseen visitor, at a safe distance. As they watched, the fruit cellar door opened and all went quiet. This experience was only the beginning of things to come.

A few days later, the couple's young daughter was away visiting relatives. The couple looked forward to some time to themselves. As they were enjoying some radio music that evening, their attention was drawn to the child's vacant room.

Her bedroom light switch flipped on and off. There were also slight noises that seemed to come from the child's room. The next event was probably the most shocking. As the couple looked on, a shadowy form came out of her room and went into the kitchen. Next, the pantry door opened up. The figure walked into the pantry and disappeared into thin air!

The couple lived in the old house for several years after the events. They loved the charm of the old place but finally moved away. The old house's history was never discovered and the reasons for the visitations remain a mystery. Perhaps the house's spiritual being continues to perform a routine they did so many times when they called the old place their home.

The Killbuck Hauntings

The *Democratic Standard* of Coshocton reported a haunting that occurred in the vicinity of Killbuck in Coshocton County. In a story dated February 1, 1889, the tragic tale unfolds.

A woman living near Sharp's Mills reported that the family was bothered nightly by sounds by feet softly treading in her home and doors slamming. Often the silence of the night was shattered by the crashing sound of what she thought to be the slamming doors. Sleep was almost impossible.

Twelve years earlier a small log cabin had occupied her house site. In it lived a Mr. David Heilman with his wife, and two young sons.

The farmer had raised a fine crop of wheat and oats but had no means to store it, so he stored it in the attic of the family home. One night, as the family slept below, the logs of the cabin separated under the great weight of the grain, and the whole crop came crashing down. Mrs. Heilman and her baby died instantly, as did the two young boys. Mr. Heilman escaped with bruises.

It was believed at the time that the footsteps were that of the wife, as she searched for something left in the old cabin. It was speculated that she was trying to communicate with someone.

As one looks back at the incident, it is possible to speculate that the loving mother is trying to find her lost children. Her last thoughts may have been of them.

The story appears to be one of those strange occurrences where the location and event seems to be the focus of the haunting, even though the old cabin is gone.

The Ghost at the Fireplace

The sight and smell of a crackling wood fire in an old fireplace, under a beautiful old mantle, is an attraction for young and old alike. We remember the stories, taffy pulls, roasting nuts and popcorn, but most of all we remember the warmth of the place, and the family members present.

An old abandoned farmhouse outside Roseville, Ohio once had such a fire and family to call its own. Hard times befell the farm and the family moved away. Later the house was rented but the tenants had little respect of love for the old place. They caused much damage before being evicted.

One of the old family members appears to have stayed with the place. Whether through undying love or some terrible accident, the apparition of a young girl or woman is said to appear beside the hearth. She often appears as little more than a shadowy form, but keeps a vigil, a reminder of times long ago.

Today (1998) the house is abandoned and in a state of disrepair. Its windows are boarded up. It represents the mere skeleton of a lifestyle that is vanishing, the small family farm.

The Ghost in the Attic

A small house on Cedar Street in Zanesville is the site of what may be called a stubborn, sometimes bothersome haunting. The trouble began when a young family moved in. From the outset, they were not alone.

The ghost in this story has an array of tricks and she is not afraid to use them. It may be that she refuses to give up her home or even share it!

She has been known to turn lights on and off, cause a phone to ring, even move items about the attic and down the stairs to the attic door. The shadowy figure has been seen against a wall and a hushed voice has been heard. It is possible she even prodded her living occupants to awaken them.

In an attempt to understand her motives, I was in the company of three individuals who decided to visit the attic. We had hoped to assist the occupants in some way.

As we entered the attic, one of my friends said, "She's right here," and pointed to a space in the floor. "She doesn't want us here as she feels this is her attic."

She went on to say that the spirit was that of a lonely old lady and that the lady might have been missing something that was important to her. The item had been in the attic. At that point my friend became nervous and said the spirit was taking a liking to her, because of the ability to communicate her feelings.

Before we departed, my other companions asked if it was possible to know the spirit's name? "I think maybe Mary Jane," was the response.

Research later that day at the county courthouse revealed a woman with the initials M. J. had lived at the house from the mid 1940's to the early 1960's.

The Victorian-Looking Visitor

A young family, struggling to make ends meet, moved into a trailer in rural Muskingum County. The last thing they expected was a nightly visitor wearing a greatcoat and old fashioned hat. It was a real worry as the visitor always made his way to the children's room, without even asking the parents' permission.

The visitation was always during the wee hours of the morning, and at first it was witnessed only by the frightened mother. She did not want to believe and at first dismissed the visitor as a dream. His visits continued.

Why would a man in a Victorian outfit be in a modern trailer? How could he get in anyway? The woman wanted answers and resolved to stay up, watch, and wait.

Sometime in the first or second hour after midnight, the man made his entrance. She sat up in bed, stunned as the man came through the door and proceeded down the hall to the children's room. Later, she questioned the children and they said the older man had visited their room and sat down in the chair and watched over them.

The woman told her spouse, who played down the event, but agreed to sit up with her. He was often not home, as he drove a truck, but the next weekend he was. The two waited into the early morning hours and the man again appeared.

This time the woman, in a loud voice, confronted the visitor. The apparition paused and then vanished before the astonished couple. Even the skeptic had to agree he had just seen something he couldn't explain, though he never called the visitor a "ghost."

The young family moved from the trailer a short time later, but never forgot their experience there. It is not known to this day why the visitor from many years past, felt the need to keep watch on the children. Perhaps something that happened in his past was the reason.

The Bakersville Incident

Sudden death is often said to produce circumstances favorable to ghost sightings. On January 1, 1881, the Coshocton newspaper called the *Coshocton Age* reported a strange incident near Bakersville in that county.

Jacob Norris, a wealthy farmer, had died after a short illness. Hardy, Mr. Norris' adopted son, took up residence in his father's old room.

The ghost of his adopted father began to appear like clockwork each Tuesday night. The ghost would enter the room and glare wildly as if searching for something, then it would depart.

Finally, young Hardy confronted the specter as to his purpose. In a low, guttural voice the spirit answered. The message was never published and was only given to one of the dead man's relatives. After that evening, the haunting never occurred again.

The Ghostly Prankster

An apartment house on Wheeling Avenue in Zanesville is the site of an unusual haunting. Occupants have reported the same activity that always takes place on cleaning day.

A man and his wife once lived together in one of the apartments. He was fond on playing tricks on cleaning day, to catch some attention from his spouse. He would take her broom and mop and hide them in the attic. She would search and search, probably with his assistance, until the hiding place was discovered.

All was not well with the man's life as he suffered from depression. One day, sadly, he chose to end his life. His wife found him dead in the bedroom, the victim of a self-inflicted gunshot wound.

Today (1998), the hide and seek game is still played! Renters have reported that the mop and broom still disappear on cleaning day and that the search usually recovers the lost items in the attic.

One young woman reports that when she moved from the apartment, she took a mop or broom with her. She thought nothing of it until one day she went to find it and it was gone! She wonders if she brought more than an old broom home, that day she moved from the apartment.

The Little Roseville Ghost

In 1967, an eight room house in Roseville was the site of a house haunting. In an upstairs bedroom the lights often came back on after being shut off. Also the blinds had a tendency to go up and down without prompting.

Once as the man of the house was downstairs watching television, he began to hear soft music. He shut the television down but the music continued. It seemed to come from upstairs.

As he climbed the stairs he began to feel he was not alone. The music continued to play, and now footsteps could be heard following him upstairs. He turned to see no one. Soon thereafter, a small figure, apparently that of a child, appeared in the doorway of the same bedroom that had been the scene of the other phenomenon.

Later, the lady of the household's mother came to visit and see what was going on. Nothing happened during her visit and a short time after that the family moved away. It appears they weren't ready to add a new member to the family, at least a ghostly one.

Who's in the Kitchen, Sis?

Do you remember the late night fright shows? How fun it was to stay up and watch those old movies. Everyone would gather around the living room and enjoy the night.

A young woman recalls growing up on Woodlawn Avenue in Zanesville, had her own late night fright show one evening. She remembers it well.

It was late in the evening and she and her sister were among those still up in the wee hours. Most of the house was dark and the light of the television lit up the room. Soon there came a sound from the kitchen. "Who's there?" There was no answer, only silence.

Attention soon went back to the movie but not for very long. Again, came the noises from the kitchen. The girls could feel cold chills going up their spines. It sounded as though someone was preparing dinner or doing dishes.

"Who's there?" came their question, this time with mounting fear in their voices. Again, there was only a dead silence to answer their question.

With much reservation, an investigation was launched. The girls crept toward the kitchen. They turned on the light; nothing was there to be seen. Again a clink came from the kitchen. The girls raced up the stairs to bed, hoping that the haunting was over and thinking to themselves; questioning what had just happened. The same events continued to reoccur, always late at night.

The girls began to think that their imaginations had got the best of them, until one dark night. As one of the girls was climbing the stairs, a dark shadowy form appeared at the top of the staircase. Fright night had become a reality!

A Formal Appearance

A lovely house, situated in a grove of pine trees on the old National Road between New Concord and Cambridge, is the site of a more formal haunting. Both ghostly inhabitants appear in uniform.

The hauntings began shortly after a new family purchased the house and began to work on it. The husband was the first to have an experience.

One evening while laying floor tile he had that feeling one gets when they are not alone. It grew stronger as he worked away, until finally he paused and looked behind him. There to his shock and consternation was the figure of a man in a dress blue military uniform, with gold emblems of some sort on his shoulders. He seemed to be supervising the work. As the husband looked on, the figure vanished. This was not the end.

The rest of the family was not to be left out. In the days that followed, the uniformed man again made his presence known, this time to the wife. On one occasion she heard footsteps, though on another, he appeared outside a room she was in. If the man in dress blues was not enough, a woman in a nursing uniform, complete with a nurse's cap, has also appeared to the family.

As 1998 begins, the story seems to continue and the mystery is yet to be solved. Are the spirits family related or left over from the previous owners of the house? At any rate, appearances must be formal.

Since the original publication it appears likely that these formal specters are related to the earlier owners. A military officer was associated with the house and it is possible that the nurse was too, possibly caring for him in later years.

Misty's Ghostly Haunted House

I lived in a house on Dryden Road in Zanesville. This house had fourteen rooms. It was an old house and kind of creepy. We soon found that we were not alone.

There were several events that happened in the old house. The first took place upstairs. When no one was upstairs, the floor seemed to come alive. The sound of children screaming and running from room to room broke the silence. Sometimes we would be sitting in our den and watching TV when plaster and paint chips would fall, flying at us from above.

I remember one frightening night when I came home and went upstairs to go to bed. I started up the first set of stairs to get to the landing and happened to look up. A woman in what looked like a white wedding gown stood before me. She was coming toward me and I didn't know what to think, other than I was seeing stuff that wasn't there. As I got closer to the woman, she came closer to me. The next thing I knew, she had walked right through me! My body had a cool sensation as if a breeze just blew straight through me.

The same night I didn't feel well. It was in winter but I was burning up, so I cracked the window and got into bed. Sleep didn't come easy that night. I had the strange feeling that someone was watching me. I looked toward the window and to my shock, there she was, the same woman, gazing into the street. She was in my room!

I didn't know what to do. I decided to talk to the owner since unusual things continued to happen. He told me one of the saddest personal stories I have ever heard. He had brought his new wife and their two children, a boy and a girl, to the house to start their life together. They had only lived there a short time when the young wife and mother, along with the two children, had been hit by a drunken driver. He'd brought them inside following the accident but each had passed away before help could arrive.

Many curious things happened in the old house but later we moved. Sometime after that, the house caught fire and burned to the ground. All that remains today (1998) is a big garage and an empty lot.

Chapter 7

More Personal Encounters and Houses

Since the publication of *Ghosts in the Valley* (1998) numerous additional stories have emerged from the darkness that sometimes surrounds these paranormal experiences. So many people have experienced things that are not easily explained. Many of the stories seem to be those of spirits that are attached to a place that meant so much to them in their lives. It is as if they don't wish to leave what is familiar to them. Are they trapped? Maybe but it seems more likely they choose to be where they are. Other cases may be more sinister.

Ghosts in the Mayor's House

An old house once sat just outside of the Putnam Historical District on the east side of Putnam Avenue. In its later years it was a rental property and had fallen into a state of disrepair. It once was the residence of Samuel Large, a mayor of the village of Putnam before it was annexed to become part of Zanesville.

A lonely looking house for many years sat vacant and boarded up on Putnam Avenue. It was an active household once and sheltered many families through the years. In 1866 it belonged to Samuel Large, Putnam's mayor.

The large, Large House seemed to be the ideal place to raise a big family. A lady rented the house with an arrangement that would allow her to purchase the property. It had been a rental and the renters had literally trashed the property when they had been forced to move. It had become a truly offensive place and it is possible that more than the living had been disturbed.

Undaunted, the lady and her children set about cleaning the place up and settling in for what she thought would be a long time. She finally had the family home she had always wanted for her kids. As a single mom, she had faced many challenges and knew there would be difficult times. She didn't think they would come from those who had lived there before. The thought had never crossed her mind.

It started with cold spots in certain rooms and locations. It was an old house; drafts she thought. But then, how does one explain the footsteps outside the rooms and on the stairs? These were heavy footsteps, slow and determined. There were a lot of kids in the house, usually about nine! The sound however was not that of scampering children and it happened at times when no one would be up. Sometimes it seemed there was an invisible presence. Most of the time, this happened when the mother was alone.

Things came to a head one night, long past midnight, when all was supposed to be quiet. Some noise, possibly the footsteps, awakened the mother and at least one of her daughters. There may have been a popping or hissing sound as the daughter caught a movement in the corner of her eye.

There was a faint blue, white glow. As the frightened girl looked on, the light became a thin mist. It began to swirl around and a blue/ white light rose up from the floor. The daughter, transfixed for the moment, soon fled the area. As soon as it had appeared, the swirling mist vanished, leaving only a cold feeling where it had been. Soon, even that was gone.

Others in the house felt an unseen presence from time to time. No one was ever harmed by the presence. Perhaps Mayor Large was just keeping watch over his household. Maybe the night visitor was a later resident of the house. We may never know. It is interesting to note that the mother's youngest son was also named Samuel.

Help Me Find My Doll

An old brick house is located near the corner of Madison Street and Putman Avenue in Zanesville. Until recently it was a rental property and owned by a long time resident of the city. Like many old houses, it could be a little scary at night with the sounds such houses can make. There were the usual creaks and cracks but on stormy nights the house became a bit more sinister.

One night the lady of the house was relaxing, listening to the pattering of the raindrops as they struck the old windows. Her mind drifted back to the day's events and events of long ago. She loved her dolls and often restored old dolls for others, so she thought about them too. She was startled from her muse, as there was a flash and a loud clap of thunder, which rattled the old windows in its fury.

The rain was intense now, the lightning sharp, and thunder seeming to explode all around the neighborhood. The pounding of the rain began to deaden and muffle everything. There was the sound of footsteps on the porch! The shadow of an old man, bent and stooped, crossed the window. She cautiously approached the door for a closer look. The man was gone! She found out later that he would often return during violent storms. It was always the same; the steps, the shadowy form of an old man and then, nothing.

Inside the old house was yet another story. Sometimes the muffled sound of a little girl playing in the upstairs was heard. She laughed and giggled, was joyful and happy. She even appeared above the steps in a pretty Victorian gown. She would look lovingly toward her living companion.

One night the little girl made an appearance outside the house in the back yard. She was digging in the ground near the clothesline. The lady watched her and wondered what she was looking for. In the morning she decided to find out.

With trowel in hand, the lady started to dig just where she had watched her little ghostly girl dig. The dirt was not too difficult to dig and soon a little hole was expanding and now was a few inches below the ground surface. There was a light ping. The lady carefully removed the dirt. It was a ceramic doll part. Soon there was another and finally two more. She had recovered the arms and legs of an old fashioned ceramic doll. The cloth body, if it was there, had long ago disappeared. The doll's head was nowhere to be found.

She believes to this day, that the little girl wanted her to find her doll and made sure she knew where to dig. Is the head there waiting to be found, or was it found a couple of lots over during an archaeological excavation? We found the head of a Mary Todd Lincoln Doll in our excavation for the Muskingum County Community Foundation some years ago. That site nearly borders the Doll Lady's house.

Does the little girl still look for this prized treasure or does she know it is in good hands? The lady has since moved away but still remembers her experiences at her house and treasures the gift the ghostly little girl pointed out to her. There is a new doll in her collection, one that will always have a special meaning to her.

A Haunted Household on Route 666

Route 666 that winds its way along the edge of the hills going north along the Muskingum River to Dresden. It has long been considered a haunted highway. Perhaps it is the significance of the number or the lonely nature of the road that snakes its way north but the road has its share of tales. Many in Zanesville refer to the dismal road as the "triple sixes." It hugs the hillside and sometimes slumps off to the river below.

At least one house that sits beside the old road seems to support the notion that "the triple or three sixes" is indeed alive with paranormal activity. It illustrates how close life and death may be related.

A young woman was visiting friends at their family home. The family had a number of small children and they needed to run a quick errand. The kids were loaded up; some in car seats and this left no room for their visitor. The young woman said that was fine and she would wait for their return.

As she sat and waited for her friends she began to feel a frigid cold come over her. It was a deep cold and it seemed to settle around and beside her. Next, a space heater came on. What a relief, except it wasn't even turned on! This was a bit unnerving, but the woman stayed in her seat, grateful to be a little warmer than before.

The space heater was humming away, the family would be home soon, but again the cold came. It was as intense as ever. Shivering, the young woman got up and made her way to the door. Once she was outside, she looked back into the house. There, before her eyes, details carved from a white, floating mist; was the figure of a husky, tall man with a moustache. His eyes seemed intent on watching her. Closing the door, she waited outside, challenging her mind to explain what she had seen. Her heart trembled, as there was no earthly explanation.

Soon the family returned to find their startled visitor. The woman asked if the family's house was haunted. "Why not that we know of," was the immediate reply. She described to them the man in detail. There was a pause before the mother spoke.

"That was the man who lived here. I took care of him until he died, there, by where you were sitting. He told me he would never leave." Apparently, he hasn't.

The Old Church Haunting

Saint Thomas Catholic Church has long served the Zanesville community. Priests and Nuns continue to perform time-honored ritual and service to the community. Many have spent most of their lives there and at least one, her afterlife.

First, the nuns noticed a presence. This happened as they walked to and from prayer, from their living quarters to the sanctuary. She was seen kneeling before the alter. At first they thought she was a visitor, someone who had come in off the street. Then again, maybe she was one of them. The nuns soon found everyone accounted for. She never spoke, but she seemed to visit frequently. She was always dressed in her Dominican habit.

As the years passed, the story was whispered about the church. It was said that a ritual was performed for her and the visits ceased for a time. Her emotional attachment seems to be strong however.

In 2001, the building was no longer being used as a residence. The nearby school used much of it for storage. Sometimes individuals still found they had business there. One, a teacher, visited the building to retrieve some needed supplies. She made her way through the cool and darkened hall to the supply room.

As she approached her destination, she saw a nun enter the hallway before her. The nun approached her quietly, looking directly at her, but saying nothing. The teacher smiled and raised her hand. She started to greet the quiet Sister who was now close enough to touch her. As the teacher opened her mouth to speak, the nun vanished, leaving only an icy chill about the hallway.

Early in 2002, two young boys found themselves in the haunted former residence. They were preparing to assist in the next service at the church. One left his book bag with his lunch box firmly attached to the frame. The boys faithfully participated in the service and returned to gather up their things.

Upon entering the room, they found the book bag in one location and the lunch box in another. Knowing something of the ghost story, they put together a plan. They brought compasses with them as they had heard that spirit activity causes compass needles to move.

As they prepared for yet another service, they watched the compass needles and began to get skeptical. Nothing was happening. Almost at the instant of their greatest doubt, the needles began to spin wildly. A timely exit from the room was in order!

When I originally typed the last two paragraphs of this story, my computer, not connected to the internet, forced me to stop typing! The Anti-Virus mechanism kicked in for no reason. That had never happened before on that computer. Enjoy the story and rest in peace!

The church remains a very active part of the community today and it is said that the nun has never left the place she loves so much.

Following Tonya

Do ghosts pay attention to the living? Are the encounters by chance, some sort of crossing of two worlds? Are our experiences brought on by chance? Why do some have a wealth of experiences and others never encounter the spirit world?

Where do I begin? I was living on Central Avenue in Zanesville, Ohio. The house just wasn't a house in the normal sense of the word. It had a presence that most were not aware of, including a friend that shared the dwelling with our family.

A visitor to the downstairs might not notice anything out of the ordinary. Ascending the stairs could put things in a different perspective. The upstairs, in the shadows, in the rooms, lurked a presence. Whatever was there, you felt it as it watched your every move.

Often as I walked upstairs, it would feel as if an incredible weight was on my back. Maybe I was tired, the steps were steep, but the experience was only beginning.

Once, deciding to take a relaxing shower, I stepped in the bathroom and locked the door. As the water cascaded over me, I felt a hand run down the center of my back! I turned with a start, to find myself completely alone. I freaked out! Again that was not the end of it.

Things began to get worse. While in bed one night, I felt something or someone in bed with me. When I pulled back the comforter, again I was alone. Sometimes the door knob to the bedroom would rattle and the door would start shaking! Two months on Central Avenue was enough.

Another time I found myself living in the country. Every night at 11 o'clock my phone would sound like it was dialing out. I decided it was best not to use my phone at that time of night. I was trying to stay on good terms with my spirit friend but sometimes things happen.

One night I was on the phone a lot longer than I expected to be. The hour of eleven came and went and I was still talking. Finally I said goodbye and sat in silence, or so I thought. Crash! All of a sudden things began hitting the floor in my kitchen! Cans of food were literally falling from my cabinets onto the floor. I never made the mistake of tying up the phone at that time again.

In May of 2002, I'm again in a house that seems to have a spirit of its own or at least one in residence. My children are afraid to go anywhere in the house alone. I'm afraid this one doesn't mean well either.

A month ago my son came running up to me, declaring that he had seen his clock run counter clockwise and reverse itself. I always feel that someone is right there with me, no matter where I am in the house. I was in the basement and heard someone just whistling away. No one was there at that time either.

My light bulbs continuously blow out. My electrical products are either broken or "on the fritz." My smoke detector chirps, even with a new battery in it.

What is most disturbing to me is the opinion of a friend who is clairvoyant. She will not step a foot in my house as she says there is too much negative energy there. It sounds like it is time to call "Ghostbusters."

The House on Rucker Road

Fultonham is a small town in Muskingum County Ohio. Located on the route of Zane's Trace, Rt. 22, it has served the early traveler, farmer and later the miner. Some who live there have done so for generations. They are very attached to their community.

A few years ago I was home alone. My husband and daughter had gone away for the evening. I had a few things to do. I finished them and sat down to relax. Resting on the couch and watching television, I noticed I was hearing some little noises. I thought it must be something outside.

There it was again. The noises were louder and I could hear what I thought were footsteps, walking across the floor upstairs. As I turned down the television, the footsteps changed. They were coming downstairs! A cold chill of fear raced through my body and I was getting goose bumps everywhere. Then the sound disappeared.

After about an hour I decided to go to bed, all the while hoping that Jim and Kandra would soon be home. I lay there awhile and finally fell off to sleep. Later, being about half asleep, I was relieved to know that Jim and Kandra were back. I felt the bed sag a little, as it always did when he sat down beside me, and soon I felt his arm around my waist. I was happy and turned to greet my husband. There was no one there to greet!

Soon I hear the familiar sound of the door opening. Kandra was there in my room. "Mom, you look like you saw a ghost!" I said, "No, I didn't see one, but... I think one was here!"

Joy still lives in her old house but will never forget that night.

Manor Ghosts

Coopermill Manor was built in the late 1930's as a public housing project for Zanesville. There are numerous legends and stories associated with the old brick apartments and have been for a number of years. There are likely even more of recent due to updating and remodeling of the rows of brick apartments.

It is said that when it was built that workers had to remove the bodies of a number of individuals from an old cemetery there. This one may not be true as the land once belonged to members of the Emery family who acquired it in the 1850's and sold it to the government for the housing project. However many things are reported that suggest that restless spirits haunt some of the buildings in the complex.

Friends and former students of mine report people sometimes hear strange sounds, like children playing in the attic storage areas. Some talk of the sounds of balls rolling or kids playing marbles. Some say they see ghostly forms in their apartments. Others dismiss the activity as imagination or "tall tales" or at least they hope they are.

My Ghostly Experience

One of my students shared her personal experience with those who are said to inhabit some of the apartments as uninvited guests. Her friend had shared the previous tale and this one didn't make her feel any better about ghosts.

I believe in ghosts because I have had an experience with one. Something happened to me at home. This is a true story. My husband and I had gone to bed one night. It had been a long day and we were pretty tired. I had not been in bed too long and I felt something take hold of my ankles. Then my body started to move up and down on the bed! I felt a rush of terror and looked over to my husband. He was sleeping soundly beside me. I tried to yell his name, only I was so scared I couldn't say anything.

I finally came to myself, poked my husband and said. "That wasn't funny!" "What are you talking about?" was his startled reply.

I told him what had happened and he thought I was crazy! He started laughing at me. I started crying. I said, "Wait till it happens to you. It won't be so funny!" He just kept laughing at me. Was I dreaming, I wondered?

The next night we went to bed and I thought I would stay awake. I waited and waited but finally fell asleep.

Later that same night my husband got out of bed. I woke up and asked him what was wrong? He looked at me and said he thought I got up and came back to bed and forgot what side of the bed I was on.

He felt someone sit down beside him, than lay down next to him. He turned in the bed to see that I was next to him, but on his other side! I had never moved the whole time. He was sharing his bed with an invisible guest, in addition to me!

My husband never again questioned me or made fun of the night the ghost grabbed "ahold" of me. After those incidents, the haunting continued. The sound of water running in the bathroom could sometimes be heard, as well as the sound of the medicine cabinet being opened.

Finally, we got rid of the bed. That was when the ghost left.

Was It Andrew?

One time, about ten years ago, when I was a little girl, we lived in the Coopermill Manor. There were five of us; my mom, sister, brother, cousin and me.

When it was bedtime, I slept with my mom. It was very late one night and I felt warm and safe by my mom. This was all to change in one startling incident. For some reason I felt someone was watching me and I looked up over the blankets.

There at the foot of our bed stood a young boy. Mom woke at that moment and thought that Andrew had come into the room to try and sleep with us. "Andrew, you know you can't sleep in here, your sister is sleeping here." By now I was anything but asleep. "Go back to your room with your cousin."

The little boy looked at her and walked from the room and vanished. It was not ten minutes later when my brother and cousin came running into the room. "There's a little boy in the room and he looks a lot like Andrew." An inspection of the boys' room revealed no little boy. Ever since then I have been scared to stay in that apartment.

Was a little boy playing a joke or was this a little lost child from another time trying to find the family he misses so much?

Chapter 8

Ghosts Along the National Road

Route 40, the old National was built through our part of Ohio in the 1830's. It followed in general, Zane's Trace from Wheeling, westward to Zanesville, where Zane's Trace split off and headed southwest. The National Road continued due west.

Originally the road was two lanes and later much of it was four lanes. It was the main east-west route across Ohio before the construction of Interstate 70. It was also the scene of many accidents and tragic deaths over its long history. The first recorded death occurred at Norwich, though no ghost story is recorded, though many others have been noted over the years. It is in a sense, a truly haunted highway!

The Ghostly Toll Keeper

Lambert Feltus for many years collected tolls along the National Road near St. Clairsville in Belmont County. Eventually the toll gate was closed but according to the Belmont Chronicle of May 15, 1890 he still wanted to collect his toll.

One rainy, misty night, Uly Smith and his "colored" wagon driver were making their way back to Wheeling. They worked for C.A. House and delivered pianos and the like about the countryside. The horse moved along at a comfortable pace until the men saw another man through the rain, standing by the road at the old toll gate site.

He stepped out, hand outstretched as the horse drew near to him. It seemed the horse passed almost through him, but the man now stood at the side of the wagon, hand outstretched, to collect the toll. "How much do you want," Uly asked? There was no reply, the old man just stood there motionless, hand still outstretched. If a coin was offered, it soon fell through the outstretched hand!

The rain was by now coming down at a good clip and the wagon driver urged his horse to do the same. They got back to Wheeling, badly shaken, but each corroborated the other's story. You see, they realized that Lambert Feltus had been dead some five years.

The Phantom Carriage

Old Washington in Guernsey County has its share of hauntings, some associated with the Civil War and others with some old residences. If one is driving through there on Route 40 at night, one might per chance meet up with one of them.

A family was driving through town late one night. As they approached an intersection they heard the unmistakable sound of slow methodic hoof beats. Who would be out after dark in a horse and buggy? Almost before they finished the thought, a buggy came out of the side street, through some mist, the driver apparently not aware of the fast approaching car.

The terrified, desperate family cringed as they waited for the shattering, splintered wood of the carriage to explode around them. There was no time to stop, it was so sudden!

The moment of impact came, and nothing. The horse, driver and carriage were gone. There was no sound, no sign that anything was ever there. It has been said that this is a reoccurring event, an image that remains of some terrible accident from many years ago.

Slow, Ghost Crossing

The National Road between Old Washington and Cambridge, Ohio is a pretty quiet place most nights. The traveler on a night journey usually has an uneventful trip.

The road that predated the current Rt. 40 was a narrow affair and as more vehicles utilized it, it was the scene of numerous accidents. Some are apparently replayed through time.

The Deep Cut, near Cambridge is one of the "Ghost Crossings." A lone figure is seen in or beside the road. The figure appears in a fog or mist and vanishes just as it is about to be hit. People call it the "Deep Cut Ghost." In some cases I have heard it reported as a headless specter, sometimes female and sometimes male. Some feel it is the ghost of a biker, killed along the road. Others report there is a young woman who appears there, maybe trying to find a ride home.

On down the highway one may encounter yet another spirit. This one is that of a man. He is said to appear on nights when a mist hangs over the road or sometimes during an autumn fog.

A man was heading home to Old Washington for the night. It had been a long tedious day and he was finding it hard to stay awake. He knew the road well but it seemed that the familiar road was one misty, white blur, against dark shadows that lined the almost vacant road. The edges of his path seemed to glow as the headlights faded into wisps of floating mist.

Something appeared to be moving, running along the road. The man snapped out of his trance-like driving mode. He was closing in on the figure at a rapid pace. His foot moved instinctively toward the brake. He felt the car start to hold back but now it was too late!

A running man appeared from out of the mist. The runner, still in front of the car, swerved desperately off the road and then, horridly, back into the path of the oncoming car. The driver braced himself for the sickening sound of his car impacting the runner. The moment was now! Silence, the victim had vanished. The encounter would never be forgotten.

In a story similar to the previous story at Old Washington, it is reported that a horse and carriage is sometimes seen in a car's rearview mirror. One minute the carriage is behind them, the next it is gone. This one occurs near Old Washington or in that town and repeats itself over the years. At any rate, maybe we need a Slow Ghost Crossing sign on the old National Road!

Antiques and So Much More

For twenty six years, Penny Court Antique Mall has been one of the places to go in Cambridge, Ohio. Located on Rt. 40, called America's Main Street, it is a great place to hunt for some old treasures to take home and enjoy. It is a place where one can take a trip back to earlier times. The past meets the present here. For many years it was a J. C. Penny department store, serving the needs of the community. Today it remains one of the most attractive storefronts in town, always worth a visit.

Penny Court is a very active place with a basement, main floor and second floor making up the shop. It can be a very active place in our physical world but also in the world of spirit.

It began when noises were heard. It was as if someone was moving things about the basement. Next, the shop cat began to stare at something in the basement and then flee upstairs for no apparent reason.

Some reported a cold chill would come over them. Collecting E.V.P. was attempted but the spirit was not talking! It was the shop camera that picked up on a vague column of mist. Another person caught an orb on film.

There was one instance that sent a chill through the owners. A loud hissing or sparking sound was heard and the owners feared a fire, but none was found. At one point the mist was loudly confronted. What happened? The mist receded into an orb like form and retreated, ducking away in the back corner of the basement.

Two young ladies wanting to see something in a locked case in the basement were talking about going upstairs to get someone with a key. They were approached by a man, well dressed in a suit. Thinking him to be an employee, they asked him to get a key to the case for them. He looked at them, as if to acknowledge their request, and turned and walked away. They waited, he didn't return. When they inquired about him, they found out that they were the only people in the basement!

There have been other incidents, and some speculate the ghostly salesman might be one of the managers that ran the department store. Apparently he maintained his office in the basement, according to an old customer, when Penny Court was J.C. Penny's.

Recently some incidents have been noted on the main floor as well. One seemed associated with an old piece of furniture, a dresser. The ghost in the basement apparently isn't ready to wave the white flag or should we say sheet. He may even have a little help from his friends!

Play Time

A house along Rt. 40, near Norwich, Ohio in a more modern subdivision has a connection to the past, possibly an old farm and a barn that remains standing. On more than one occasion young children have been spotted apparently playing in the yard. These spiritual kids have also been seen holding hands and walking in a line into the barn.

The children are seen, but sometimes heard as well. They laugh and giggle; sometimes the happy sounds of children playing come to one's ears. The children seem locked in their own world, oblivious to the world of the living. The house is modern and appears to be unrelated to the activity.

The owners have noted some rough play late at night. It seems to come from the bathroom area of the house and sounds like people fighting and possibly breaking things. With all the commotion, nothing has ever been found damaged or broken. It seems to be like some moment frozen in time, some energy imprint, not unlike a photograph of a time long ago.

The Cabin Ghost

One of the towns along the old National Road was Norwich. Today it is bypassed by the more modern Rt. 40. The National Road was known for its restaurants, motels and in the earlier days its taverns and inns. Sometimes private residences would also offer rooms and meals to the weary travelers. A number of the buildings remain today but most are no longer used for their original purpose.

A small log cabin in the town of Norwich, Ohio once served as a residence and a restaurant. The cabin fell into disuse for most visitors but apparently not one particular visitor. People have reported a misty looking figure, usually just a glimpse of him. He wears an old fashioned, long great coat and a hat, resembling a cowboy hat. He might rapidly move across the doorway and vanish from sight.

Later, with the restaurant closed, a passerby noticed a red glow in the windows. The first thought was that the old building was on fire. Looking in the window, the astonished traveler saw the red glow glimmering from a non-burning fireplace. There was the same man, standing over the phantom fire, the red glow shimmering off his long coat and hat. As the visitor observed the man and the fire, the scene vanished.

The stranger is still said to haunt the old building and no explanation has ever been offered as to what binds him to that place. Does this haunting represent the end of one man's journey, or simply an attachment to a place that touched his heart?

So many stories and events are associated with the historic National Road, U.S. Rt. 40. It is no wonder that so many ghost stories are a part of its heritage. So much remains to be discovered. Much of the road remains intact and many of the side roads actually represent some of the earliest segments. As you travel this road, explore the forgotten parts. Who knows what may be waiting for you around the next bend.

Chapter 9

Witchcraft and Demon Creatures

Most people believe that witchcraft and demonic creatures are the stuff of Halloween. Witchcraft was very real to some of the early settlers, as were creatures that were hard to explain. Early in this book we explored some of the early stories. It is somewhat remarkable to note that old beliefs and stories persist in today's oral traditions, and that some forms of witchcraft are practiced today. The stories, though hard to find, lurk in the Muskingum Valley.

Back to Nature

Humans, no matter where you find them, no matter what culture, in their earliest state were totally dependent on nature. Whether dependent on the hunt or the harvest, the people recognized the need to be close to the natural environment. There were always things that could not easily be explained, especially in times of trouble and at the same time there had to be a reason for celebrations. There were always questions that needed answers.

Often times, animals with certain characteristics, were considered magical, sometimes good; sometimes bad. They became totems to be revered but also scape goats for everything that went wrong. The owl was one such creature. Being nocturnal, it was mysterious. In some cultures it is considered wise, a messenger, watching over the night; while in others it was a stealer of souls, used by evil witches. Appalachian folk tales state that if a hoot owl roosts in your yard for several nights, it means there will be a death in the family. Others might say it is keeping evil away, protecting you.

The Opossum in North America is considered a magical animal by a number of Native American tribes. The fact that it can fain death and then revive, lent to its mysterious nature. Again it was nocturnal, from a world not often considered safe for humans. Its clinging tale and the fact it carried its young in a pouch made it different, not to mention its musk and a mouth full of sharp pointed teeth, exposed when it would hiss. It was another messenger, possibly keeping watch for someone. What was its intention, living near camp?

Bears were sometimes considered to be humans, who had grown tired of their lives and wandered into the woods, changing to Bears! Cats, especially black ones, were often considered familiars of witches. They were the vehicle by which the witch communicated with Satan. During the Bubonic Plague in Europe, they were sometimes thrown over the castle walls and into moats as they were blamed for spreading the sickness or had failed to protect the household from the flea carrying rats. Finally, snakes are frequently killed for just being themselves though the reason in many cases is that they are supposed to represent evil. The devil took the form of the serpent. At the same time the snakes entwined around the medical staff represent doctors!

Finally, Sasquatch comes to mind. The creature exists in many oral traditions throughout the world, though we are yet to find it. In our area it was likely a part of the Delaware/Lenape tradition. It was considered the guardian or the keeper of the animals, especially deer. A Fall Festival was held in its honor, to insure the animals would be kept close to camp during the often cruel winter months, when the line between sickness and health, life and death was much less defined.

Witchcraft

A few years ago, bottle diggers in Putnam uncovered a rare and unusual discovery. They found a Witch Bottle in an 1850's privy. The bottle containing shoe leather, embedded with pins and needles, and filled with a liquid, probably urine, had been deposited in its final resting place. Why was this made and what was its use?

The owner had used this "trick" to ward off evil, if he was following the old world tradition. The bottle was a counter to the presumed curse of a witch. Why was it in the privy, intact? Was it just discarded or was it there because of some possible affliction affecting the user.

Today some beliefs have remained throughout the Muskingum Valley. One person I interviewed told me of some old practices that remain with us. She stated that if you want two people to always be together, you cut out two figures and paste them together, hiding the pasted figures away.

Another belief that persists is beating an old rug. If one beats an old rug supposedly while cursing or shouting a person's name, it is supposed to physically harm the person, as if they are being beaten.

Sometimes it is hard to tell genuine activity from pranks or vandalism. Pentagrams are said to be used in traditional rituals yet today. They also manifest themselves in some pop culture. They were supposed to protect the participant as certain rites and rituals were preformed, often with candles burning at the star points on a floor but they also find themselves as wall decorations and jewelry!

It is interesting to note that many animal shelters won't allow black cats to leave the shelters at Halloween, due to the chance they will be mistreated or even sacrificed. The black cat is still looked at as unlucky or even a "familiar" - used in communicating with the devil. More often, they could be the victims of pranks and cruelty at Halloween. In 2018, their fortunes appear to have changed. The movie, Black Panther, has resulted in a spike in black cat adoption and the shelters have few in house.

The Greenwood Demon

The house was large and gloomy looking at first impression. The family was excited about getting the house. Even the daughter, who had a melancholy feeling about the place, was excited about it. The parents loved the old place and before long everyone was settled in.

Soon, lights began to go on and off, doors would open and shut and the daughter thought that maybe they had a friendly ghost, like "Casper." Then everything seemed to change.

The family was a Christian family and very church oriented but soon the mother's personality began to change. She pulled away from the church, showed symptoms of mental illness and became abusive. The father seemed to lose contact with everything and everybody and began to live alone.

One day the daughter came home to find her mother on the phone, discussing a dark, cloaked figure with terrifying eyes. She was telling how it was staring at her from the alley, mocking and laughing at her.

The daughter's face could not hide the terror, for she realized she had seen the same thing in her in her own bedroom. They believed it to be a demon. Their pastor shared their opinion.

The next day the pastor arrived and an attempt was made to force the demon out of the house. The mother, daughter and pastor held hands and prayed.

As the group prayed, strange voices were heard upstairs. The pastor went from room to room, praying and sprinkling blessed water. They heard screaming and doors opened and closed. Next was heard the sound of a strong wind blowing but none was felt. The air became incredibly thick.

When the pastor left, things settled down for a while. Some years later, the mother died at the house. To this day, the daughter believes that her mother was possessed. The house is still there (1998) and is rented out but no one seems to stay there very long. Does the Greenwood Avenue Demon still haunt the old house or was it banished forever?

The Chesterhill Demon

The village of Chesterhill is situated on a ridge top in Morgan County. The area was originally settled by Quakers and many persons of color, most being a mix of African, Native American and European blood. They brought with them many rich traditions.

Several years ago, a story surfaced from the farmland and forest surrounding Chesterhill. The incident took place in the late fall of the year around the time of the Hunter's Moon.

A young man entered the woods with his two fine hunting dogs. He had decided that the night was right for hunting raccoons. He wasn't far in the woods when his dogs picked up a scent. Off they went, bounding into the darkened woods. The sound of their baying was a joy to the young hunter.

Within a mile or two the sound changed to that of hounds that had treed their quarry. As the hunter approached, all went suddenly quiet.

The hunter asked himself, why had all the sounds, including that of the dogs suddenly ceased? Then near the foot of a large, old tree, he spotted the shaking, quivering form of one of his hunting dogs. The other had vanished.

The hunter cautiously peered into the tree branches with his small miner's lamp. A great terrifying set of eyes glowed in the night. All seemed to go black and then what seemed like thousands of pairs of glowing eyes lit up the night. The giant set in their midst. With a sudden cracking and crashing or branches, something was coming down. The hunter emptied his gun; still the crashing continued.

The young man fled in terror, just as a giant form jumped from the tree. The hunter managed to load his weapon and fire as he ran. The shots were wild and most of the shells fell to the ground along the path of his desperate retreat.

Stumbling and staggering, the young hunter managed to stay just ahead of the creature in pursuit. The creature, being larger than his prey, continued to crash through the woods, chasing after the man. Just before he reached the clearing and the road, the man staggered and nearly fell. As he leaped from the woods, there was a terrible burning sensation and pressure on his back. He thought death had come to claim him.

As he fled the scene, the burning sensation stayed with him. Upon reaching home, quickly removed his shirt and ran cold water on his back.

There, in the middle of his back, was what appeared to be a giant, red print of a human-looking hand. It was at least twice the size of a normal hand, and burned into his back, like a grotesque sunburn.

He returned to the site of his trial the following day. He visited the site in broad daylight, with a pastor friend. The path he had run looked like a great storm had been through it. Small trees and bushes were broken and his ammunition was scattered about. Of his prized hunting dogs, one was never found and the other was never the same.

The young hunter resolved to never hunt that part of the forest again. He was convinced he had met the Chesterhill Demon. To this day (1998) he has kept that resolution. The area today remains very wild and remote, a place where someone might easily disappear.

The Powelson Creature

In 1971, the following story was being told in the Zanesville vicinity. It concerned a demonic creature that was said to inhabit an old coal mining area just north of Zanesville and south of Dresden, Ohio.

The creature is said to be associated with an old neglected cemetery, along a lane that takes off from a wildlife area access road and leads to the graveyard. It has been spotted in the woods, in rugged terrain, and along the lane at night. Its victims were said to be young lovers who enjoyed parking in the area. Many were said to have been terrorized by this apelike, ghostly looking creature that seemed to be able to appear and vanish at will.

One night a couple was parked in the old lane, enjoying some romantic moments together when they thought they heard something. A moment later the creature came through the brush and banged against the vehicle! In terror, the young man slammed the car into reverse and the vehicle plunged backward toward the safety of the road. As it did, an ear piercing scratching sound was heard. The couple sped away into the night, headed for home. When they got there, they found a metal hook like weapon jammed into the car's door.

Is this story one that was experienced by the terrorized couple or simply an urban legend, used to frighten your girlfriend, so the two of you could get a little closer on a cold autumn night? We may never know but it remains today a part of the ghost lore of our region. Often repeated, it persists.

Rosemary Street

Ron and some friends had heard a lot of stories about an old abandoned house on Rosemary Street in Zanesville. One night they decided to find out if the stories were true.

Some friends and I had heard a lot of stories about a house on Rosemary Street in Zanesville being haunted. So one night we decided we were going to see if we could get into the house. It was pretty late at night when we got there. We parked just down the street and walked up to the house.

It was surrounded by woods so we tried the front way. When we got to the house we were already hearing strange noises. We looked up, and standing in the doorway was a very large figure. It looked like the shadow of a man, but there was no face or anything. We ran from the front of the house, and gathered back together down on the street.

We then decided to try the side entrance to the house. We knew no one lived there; the place had been boarded up for years. We thought maybe we were just seeing things before.

When we got to the side of the house, you could see two windows at the corner of it. The windows should be to the same room but you could see a light in only one of them. The house had no electricity, so you shouldn't be able to see any light at all. As we were standing there, the dark figure appeared at the window, like it didn't want us in the house. We ran again.

Looking back, we were pretty brave, or at least we thought so, and didn't give up! We decided to try one more time. This time we would approach from the back of the house.

We went up to the alley behind the house and started down through the woods. We got about halfway down to the house and out of nowhere there was a huge black dog in the middle of the woods. It sounded mean and was coming after us fast. We ran out to Mershon Road. As soon as we got out of the woods, the huge black dog was gone.

We all met once again on Rosemary Street. We decided we were done trying to explore the old house. I looked to my left and right, the other guys were running away. I turned back to my left and there was a woman in a long black night gown, coming right toward me. It looked like she was floating, not walking. You couldn't see her face either.

It scared me so bad I ran and beat the other guys back to the car. That woman wasn't there the first time I had looked to the left! The next house was clear at the end of the block, so she didn't come from there either.

I just know someone or something wanted to keep us out of that old, boarded up, abandoned house. It worked, we never tried again.

Occurrence on Eastman Street

Some stories seem a bit too unusual, but none the less, they are still part of the ghost lore of our area of Ohio. This story is one of those.

A rental property on Eastman Street in Zanesville had gotten the reputation of being haunted. There was no record of a tragedy there but it was said that years ago, people went there and preformed secret rituals. Bells could be heard at times, ringing for no reason and if one listened, strange chanting could be heard within the house.

One man at the house felt a strange burning sensation in his pocket but there was no smoke or fire. He reached into his pocket, finding a dime, bent into a "U" shape and still hot. The mystery was never solved.

Witchcraft at Old Washington in 1809

William Wolfe, in his *Stories of Guernsey County*, published in 1943, is one of the few historians that consider oral traditions about witchcraft and ghosts worthy of consideration. I have included two of his stories in summary form in this publication (1998).

Sometime before 1943, an old structure was raised in Old Washington. The house was said to date to 1805. As the house came down, horseshoes were found nailed to the log walls of the structure. They were numerous and enclosed the living space. Also, a jug of whiskey was found, placed securely between two logs. The townsfolk wondered what this might mean. One of the oldest residents of Guernsey County provided the answer. He recalled as a child in 1809, that a witch scare had hit the village. Doctors had found it impossible to treat a young child in the village. The boy responded to nothing.

Shellbrick Wirr, a self-proclaimed "witch doctor," pronounced that the child was bewitched. A woman near the village was accused of bewitching the child. She was seized and a bizarre treatment was administered.

Wirr said the only way the child could be cured was to burn holes in the thighs of the accused witch. A red hot iron was applied to the witch and the child was seen to improve.

Shellbrick Wirr wasn't finished yet. He stated that the house was still bewitched and this is why the horseshoes were mounted on the walls and the whiskey placed between the logs.

Another belief that persisted at that time was the belief that if you shot the picture of a witch with a silver bullet, and she was guilty, she would soon die.

Muskingum County Witchcraft

In the early nineteenth century, the belief in witchcraft still persisted in the minds of many citizens. We are not talking of the religion that celebrates the linking of the human spirit with nature but a more malevolent form of magic, that of the dark side.

Norris Schneider, in an article for the *Times Recorder* of October 31, 1976, recalled an incident that occurred in Roseville. It concerned a citizen of that community, Mary Rose.

Joe Clark came to Roseville and set up the first tavern and hotel there. He soon fell sick. The neighbors watched to see what would happen to the unfortunate man. As he neither died nor recovered, it was assumed he was bewitched.

Clark said there would be no way to cure him unless he shot the witch with a silver bullet. He decided to attempt an experiment.

A silver bullet was made from a twelve and a half cent piece, and rammed it into a rifle. The profile of a witch was drawn in charcoal on the side of his house. A crowd assembled to watch the tavern keeper. Joe went into the street, took aim and fired. The profile of the witch was struck in the leg.

Mary Rose, the wife of Ezekiel Rose, immediately went lame in the same leg as was shot in the charcoal profile. This to the townspeople identified the witch and there was a storm of protest against her. The Roses found they could no longer live near Roseville.

Joe Clark got well, but from then on, people were said to tell stories of Mary Rose's power as a witch.

In 1898, a story was published in the Zanesville area about Mr. and Mrs. Isaac Murry of Columbia Street. They claimed to be bewitched for twenty years. The evening hours were sometimes filled with rapping sounds and the couple experienced visions. In one instance Mr. Murry instructed his wife to strike at the spirits with a sword. The forms took the shape of humans, cats and dogs.

The couple claimed that they had seen over one hundred snakes in one room of their house. They turned and twisted all over the floor. Witches were said to slap their faces until the couple was black and blue.

The lady stated that some protection was obtained by carrying a lit candle into a darkened room. She also talked of using salt and magic chants to ward off evil. Never, though, did they identify their nemesis.

This incident is one of the latest to be published concerning the practice of witchcraft occurring in the Muskingum Valley. It was recorded in the *Zanesville Weekly Courier* of March 10, 1898. It is one of the most unusual incidents published in a newspaper I have seen.

The Pentagram

The pentagram is essentially a five pointed star. It is associated with magic and witchcraft but it means many different things, depending on religion and culture. Christians often believe it represents the five wounds of Jesus. Wiccans and other groups feel it can have various meanings from representing our human nature to symbols of the world and creation.

It can be considered a symbol of order and chaos. Three points up represents the order of things in the world, and "white" magic, while two points up represents the world order turned upside down, or "black" magic. Two points up is also the symbol of the goat, using its horns to prod at the heavens! Two points up is also the symbol of the Church of Satan. At the same time, the Eastern Star, women associated with the Masonic Orders, have a pin with the star, two points up! Their projects often help people in the community.

I can recall only two instances where I saw it drawn out for use, both on paranormal investigations. One was in the attic of a house and the other was in the ballroom of Prospect Place, many years ago. In the second case, the burnt wax of candles was noted at each point of the star. Was someone or group seeking to communicate with the devil or was some other ritual involved? Was it someone only out to scare their partying friends?

Halloween at Paden House p. 77 (G.Felumlee, 2018)

The Ballroom at Prospect Place, Trinway, Ohio

Apparition of a Young Woman in White (Middle Right) p.69

(Gary Felumlee, 1992)

Dancing Orbs! We were playing Civil War Music at Prospect Place. P.69

(Gary Felumlee, 2018)

The Stone Academy, Zanesville, Ohio p.47

No one was in the building when this was taken, note face in window.

(Gary Felumlee, 2018)

The Opera House, McConnelsville, Ohio p.56

(Gary Felumlee, 2018)

Site of the Buckeye Belle Explosion, Beverly, Ohio p.18

(Gary Felumlee, 2018)

Chapter 10

Unusual Possibilities

Some stories are found in the oral traditions of our area and in many cases are passed down, and sometimes the details change over time as well. The first one was recorded in a 1903 newspaper article in Zanesville, the others are oral traditions sometimes passed from generation to generation. Each has its merits and is a part of the history of the Muskingum Valley.

Jack the Bluffer

Halloween time in Putnam in 1903 took a strange twist. Besides the usual pranks of Gate Night (Taking Gates of the Hinges), placing a buggy on a barn roof or, and this one is nasty, moving the outhouse behind the hole, a strange looking, ragged man began to appear to the ladies of Putnam. He came to be called, Jack the Bluffer.

Typically, after the man of the house had left for the day or the evening, Jack the Bluffer would appear inside of the home. He would show the lady of the house a filthy looking note demanding money. Upon receiving a coin or two, the man would step outside and seem to vanish. To this day, Jack the Bluffer remains a mystery. Was he a prankster, a hobo, or something else entirely?

Black Joe

Ghosts, or the threat thereof, are sometimes used to scare little ones into better behavior. Black Joe was said to roam the streets of old Putnam in Zanesville, looking for little boys and girls who didn't return home when they should.

As the shadows and darkness of night fell, Joe was said to be peering from behind old trees that lined the streets. His black shadow was said to fall on the sidewalks. Some feel Black Joe might be the ghost of the slave in the story, the Runaway. Others thought he was nothing more that the shadows projected from the old trees that lined Putnam's streets.

Burles on the sides of some of the old maples would cast head-shaped shadows, heightening the child's fear and sending him or her home at a more rapid pace.

The Tanner's Dog

H.C. Howells was a leather tanner from England, living in Putnam in the 1830's. He was one of the founders of the Abolitionist Movement in Putnam. Howells had seen the slave trade and was noted for his fiery speeches against slavery.

In 1839, a mob attacked the Stone Academy as it had in 1835. They threatened the abolitionist speakers with serious harm. After the meeting at the Stone Academy was broken up, the mob went in search of H.C. Howells at his home. They planned to tar and feather him or at the very least assault him and his property.

Howell's was tipped off and was hiding on Putnam Hill, tradition says in a hollow tree. The mob, finding Howells not at home, took its anger out on his dog. The mob hanged it in his yard. The pitiful little dog struggled and kicked as it was strangled to death.

Some say that rustling bushes and soft padded footsteps heard in this neighborhood, late in the evening, are those of the Tanner's dog, still looking for his master.

Wally Moore, a local Putnam and Muskingum River historian and I were talking one day before he passed and he asked me, "Did you see that little black dog down by the river?" He smiled.

In the late 1920's and early 1930's, Wally recalled hanging out near the river with his friends. It wasn't uncommon for one of the group to say, "Did you see that dog running around over there?" The reply was, "What dog?"

The little ghost dog was said to haunt the cemetery and the river bank area. Wally exclaimed, "That story haunted more than a few little kids!"

The Mounted Corpse

A story that has persisted over a number of years and still survives today in 2018 is that of a bizarre burial in Moxahala Burying Ground. The tale talks of a man that so loved his horse that he was buried with it.

Apparently, one of his last wishes was said to be that the grave be dug so deep that the horse could stand or crouch in it! The man's body would than sit atop is horse! Alexander Fluke, the caretaker of the burial ground would be hand digging in river gravel to accomplish that. People none the less said "Yes this was true."

Again, Wally Moore takes up the tale. "Me and some boys were playing in the old burying ground. Most of the stones were gone even back then. There was one grave that was humped up above the ground. We were using it as a bicycle ramp. A couple of stones gave way, and we looked inside. There was a skeleton, lying on its back with a lot of open space around it."

The grave remained open for a couple of days and local people came to see this early settler. The newspapers got into an argument as to what to do about the situation and the curiosity seekers. One of the boys put a stick into the grave and retrieved the skull, though Wally made him put it back. They found no horse!

The grave is that of Calvin Conant, an early doctor in Putnam. It was constructed in the form of a Masonic Arch, thus the shape. This grave was disturbed twice, once a generation before Wally where some boys played cards over the doctor's skeletal remains, using his chest as the table. A side light to this event is that it was some of the doctor's students that robbed a grave in this very cemetery, planning to learn their trade on a young girl named Annie. It seems when it comes to disturbing graves, what goes around, comes around, at least at Moxahala Burying Ground.

As to horses in burials, I have heard of the practice in some western Native American traditions. The story here seems to be because of the arch construction which rises above the ground level of the cemetery. So far, there is no horse to be found at Moxahala Burying Ground, but paranormal activity; that may be quite another matter.

"Quit You Old Devil" The Fye and Barr Stoning

Morgan County has two stories that seem to fit the Unusual Possibilities category. Both involve "stoning" of wooden structures and were blamed by some on ghosts or possibly evil doings by demonic hands.

Two Morgan County homes were subjected to stoning, one in 1916 and the other in 1869. The cases were never explained to everyone's satisfaction and both are subject to a fair amount of skepticism. The incident in 1916 made a number of newspapers.

Unusual incidents began to happen on the Fye farm in 1916, according to Norris Schneider in an article published in the *Times Recorder* on April 9, 1978. At first, cows were "blanketed" or covered with feed sacks. Later, horses were turned around backwards in their stalls.

Then, a rain of stones began from the nearby hillside. Stones, some very large in size, would roll down the hill and hit the sides of the Fye barn. One large boulder broke through the side of the barn. Another stone, nearly hit Mrs. Fye. She hollered at the top of her voice, "Quit you old Devil!" The Fyes had to keep replacing boards as the damage continued.

One startled neighbor, standing guard with a shotgun, saw a yoke and harness break through the barn's side. The largest boulder that hit the building was thirty-six pounds in weight. Eventually the stoning ceased.

Interestingly enough, one of the Fye boys had come to Zanesville some weeks before the incidents made the newspapers. He had told a number of friends the same story. Some felt the boy had a hand in the pranks, though he never did admit it. The story caused quite a stir, especially around nearby Merriam Station.

The *McConnelsville Conservative* of September 14, 1869 reported a similar incident at the Barr home: "The stoning commenced on Friday, August 27th and continued until the following Tuesday." The home showed damage from the stones, including three broken window panes. The largest stone to strike the house was six and three-fourths pounds.

The Barr's daughter was suspected of doing the deed and was restrained and watched over. The stoning continued. Though no one was ever shown to have done the deed, a human prank was still suspected. Did the Fye boy of 1916, perhaps read of the 1869 events in an old newspaper? At any rate, some say Morgan County ghosts like to throw rocks.

A Night Journey

Imagine for the moment the beauty of a full moon as its reflection sparkles off the ripples in the water of the Muskingum River. You make your way alone, through the soft glow of moonlight, down a well-used trail to Marietta. Everything seems peaceful as your horse moves through the beautiful nightscape. Your thoughts turn to home or maybe your lover or someone you haven't seen for so long. Cares seem to disappear, swallowed in the sparkling pools and falls in the river.

Major Horace Nye, one of the earliest settlers of the Muskingum Valley, had grown up in the early settlements in the valley. He was one of a number of men who had worked the salt springs near Chandlersville. Later, and for most of life, he had been a resident of Putnam.

Sometime after the War of 1812, when the danger of Indian attack was no longer an issue in the valley, settlement of the region began in earnest. It was commonplace to travel between Putnam and Marietta. One moonlit night, Major Nye set out on an eagerly anticipated night journey.

It is impossible to know, but Nye's thoughts probably drifted back to the early days as he remembered familiar landmarks, now bathed in the blue-white light of the moon. So much was changing in his beloved valley. He may have entered the hill country, still sparsely settled, and traveled the Old Saltmakers' Road near Chandlersville.

It was near midnight and the major whistled to keep himself company as he made his way toward Marietta. The night was beautiful but it had become so still. The whistling continued as the horse and rider passed below a vaguely outlined hilltop.

Suddenly there came an unearthly scream from the hill above him! He threw up a hand to catch his hat as his hair stood on end and his horse reacted to the unearthly sound. The sound was nothing like anything he had heard before. It was a horrifying cross between a woman, a baby and a beast. He now realized he had no weapon, save for a small whip. There would be no more whistling that night. He urged his horse along, quickly leaving the source from where the sound had originated. What was up there and what might lie in wait for his return?

Was the sound that of a panther or perhaps an owl or just maybe something else? There is no doubt the major was not alone on his moonlit night journey to Marietta. Sometimes a night of peace and solitude can be shattered when one encounters the unexpected. Major Horace Nye was not a man afraid of danger. In 1839, in his later years, he stood at the 3rd Street Covered Bridge with his War of 1812 musket and said, "Did someone say shoot?" as anti-abolition rioters came across the bridge from Zanesville to attack the Putnam abolitionists and threaten to burn their village. Never the less, that night on the road to Marietta, was one he never forgot.

The Spirit of Indian Hills

The site of the Maysville High School complex in 2018, off Moxie-Darla Road some 1200 plus years ago was the site of an Indian village or hunting camp, as evidenced by the worked flint that has been found there in the past.

It is located near two or possibly three ancient mounds that were often sacred burial places for the dead in those ancient times.

A few years ago, probably in the fall of the year, a group of students were having a bonfire and wiener roast at a nearby trailer court. This was located near one of the mounds and from the hill it might look as though it was on or near the mound.

The night progressed and as people often do, one person left the camp fire area. Wandering off in the direction of the hill and old cornfield, the student was swallowed up by the night shadows. He began to feel very alone. Hesitating for a moment, he heard the dry leaves rustle and crack behind him. Fear and suspicion crept over him as did a cold night breeze.

Before he could turn around to see who or what might be behind him, he felt a touch on his shoulder. His heart was pounding hard now and he turned to see only his friend behind him. The party was wrapping up and his friend had come to get him. As they stood together, both noticed a movement upon the hill. Again there was a feeling of dread beginning to rise up as they studied the hill above.

Their eyes saw the dim outline of a human figure, maybe somebody had gone up there to give them a scare! They devised a plan to wait for the prankster.

"We'll turn the tables on him, let's wait and watch!" they said. The figure was now making its way down the hill toward the glow of the fire. It seemed to move slow and haltingly, as though it was an elderly man. An eerie glow of light highlighted the form that was approaching them. It was now close enough to make out detail and the tables were about to turn!

The students' hearts skipped a beat. They wanted to run, but stood transfixed! The figure was that of an aged Indian, dressed in skins and furs of wild animals. The ghost was almost upon them! Just as the students were about to break into a panicked flight, the image disappeared.

Old timers will tell you that Indian spirits still roam the hill and surrounding countryside. In ancient times, burials were often made in houses that were burnt down over the corpse. Some bodies were dismembered and cremated in ceremonial fires. Was the spirit attracted to the mound or fire? Was he a shaman, assigned to dismember the body or did the students witness the last moments of an old warrior or chief? One thing is certain; it was a night that wouldn't soon be forgotten. Next time the fire should be by invitation only. But then again, what would be the fun of that?

Legends of Egypt Valley

Egypt Valley is a remote wilderness area in Belmont County, Ohio. Today, much of it is a wildlife area. The area, before the days of coal mining and the Gem of Egypt dragline, was dotted with small farms. In Kirkwood Township, a small lonely cemetery seems to be a center of activity, though I have not been there personally. Unusual events are reported at the cemetery but also in the surrounding area, the wilderness in general.

One historical fact about the early history of the area was the murder of Louiza Catharine Fox by Thomas Carr on January 21, 1869. I learned of the story from a local reporter. She was interested in paranormal activity and shared this account.

It was a dark, somewhat dreary night a few years ago, when a young woman and her friend drove into Egypt Valley. Their goal was to visit the grave of Louiza Fox. They hoped to see the young girl as she wanders the woods. The valley was a foreboding place at night. The visitors had the feeling that things weren't right. The feeling seemed to intensify until it was almost overwhelming.

There were strange mists that seemed to rise up and move through the trees. Were these restless spirits or just ground fogs? Then they caught a glimpse of what seemed to be lights or small fires back in the woods. Finally they reached the old graveyard. Salem Cemetery was a lonely and dismal place and the feeling of an unseen presence, just watching them, got even stronger.

They were beginning to regret their night's adventure and feeling it was time to go.

The friends wasted no time in leaving. As they left, what appeared to be a ball of fire, whose flames illuminated the night, was seen burning in the top of a barren tree. It had turned out to be an evening, a special one that neither will ever forget.

It is said that Louiza Fox continues to roam the woods of Egypt Valley. Some believe a number of witches are buried in unmarked graves in Salem Cemetery. It is whispered that if one walks around the edge of this cemetery six times, they will vanish! One fact is clear, Louiza Catharine Fox is buried there in Egypt Valley but does she truly rest there?

No Skeletons in the Closet, What's in the Attic?

Woodlawn Avenue in the Historic Putnam District of Zanesville, Ohio has its share of hauntings and potential hauntings. One strange incident took place a few years ago. It may be an example of the dark side of Putnam, over one hundred years ago.

Many of the large houses in the Putnam Historic District were built by prominent families throughout the 1800's and into the earliest 1900's. A good number of these citizens were successful business men and leaders in the community there. Their social status was very important to them and they would go to extreme lengths to preserve it. Social status was very important in Victorian and Edwardian times.

What if one of their daughters was involved in a relationship, outside of marriage, had a child or children, and they died at childbirth or shortly thereafter? Sometimes the newspapers of that time talk of dead newborns being found by the river. How would one of these prominent families deal with such a situation?

A story has circulated around Putnam for a few years that one of the houses on Woodlawn Avenue had a collection of tiny occupants. What might they be?

A young man who had some training in woodwork, house construction, and remodeling as well as restoration was acting as a consultant for a couple of prospective home buyers. They wanted to purchase a large, structurally sound historic home. It was his job to inspect it from top to bottom.

All went well with the inspection and the young man made his way to the attic. Armed with a small flashlight, he peered into the darkness. The floors looked good and solid; there were no roof leaks, insect damage or rotting wood to be seen. Something seemed stuffed between the floorboards and roof; he thought he should take a look.

Bending down low to the floor, he approached what looked like a pile of old rags with something possibly in it. Shining his light against the dusty cloth, he saw three tiny shriveled up looking heads, staring back at him! They appeared dry, dusty and mummified in the dimming light of his flashlight. In terror he staggered back from the site. In his mind he was looking at three dried and mummified babies. Had he found a young woman's secret and a family's shame?

He told the buyers of his discovery but was never quite sure of what he saw; three opossums, three old dolls or the unthinkable, three newborn infants. He never returned to the house.

Chapter 11: Cemeteries - The Final Chapter

Sometimes!

This chapter takes us to the final resting place but certainly not the end of the story. Cemeteries have often been the subject of ghost stories and paranormal activity. Here are a few samples of this "bill of fare." Remember if you visit or investigate cemeteries, always treat them with respect and follow any posted rules. There is much history to be found there and often beautiful examples of cemetery art, and symbolism, connecting our world to the next.

Darla's Greenwood Cemetery Story

It was a dark night. I was ten years old. My mother and father were visiting my aunt and uncle. My cousin Kathy and I were best friends and playing outside. My aunt and uncle lived in the caretaker's house in Greenwood Cemetery in Zanesville and we had plenty of room to play.

On this particular night we decided to walk down through the cemetery. It was spooky and the sky was darkened by the coming night. The trees hanging over the road were moving from a steady breeze there on the hill. We were a little scared but that was the thrill of walking at night. We often did it to have fun.

We came to the large mausoleum. The door was open. We debated as to whether we should enter or not. Being the curious kids we were, we walked in. We had a little light shining through the door, a moon glow from the rising moon. We saw something white, glowing in the corner. As we turned to run, the door slammed shut. We were terrified to look at what might be behind us. We just kept talking to each other and trying to calm each other down.

After what seemed like hours, we saw my other cousin, David, walking through the cemetery. He liked to look for bats and throw rocks at them.

We saw a greenish mist that seemed to come from a vault. We screamed for David repeatedly. He came to the door or our temporary horrible prison and we told him we were locked in. He went up to the house and got the key from my uncle. We were saved!

From that night on, we just played ball in front of the house.

Homemaking, Greenwood Cemetery Style

Bonnie wasn't always fond of it but sometimes a walk through Greenwood Cemetery was kind of exciting. It was getting dark one evening and Bonnie decided to take a walk with her uncle and cousin. Trees were becoming dark shadows against a rapidly fading sky. The tombstones began to take on more sinister shapes and a deep quiet was falling over the party of walkers. The road winding through the sprawling, lonely graveyard remained dimly lit. One thing was certain, not another living soul was around.

Passing through the old stone arch with a cast iron gate, the group made their way to the caretaker's house. When it had been occupied, unusual things had been said to have happened there. Appliances would turn on and off, and the television would change channels by itself. Some heard strange sounds and others claimed to see mists. The group passed the old house and went deeper into this final, "resting place," for so many of Zanesville's citizens.

The large gray mausoleum, site of Darla's experience, loomed before the trio. As they were about to pass and continue on their walk, a movement caught their straining eyes. They turned toward the massive tomb and no one said a single word. The sight that greeted them; none would ever forget.

A white figure was walking inside the mausoleum. It was walking in a circle and appeared to be sweeping. Next thing the figure did was come through the front door to the sidewalk outside. We didn't say a word but we all saw it.

The figure, looking like a white shadow, was that of a woman with very long hair. She was a little heavy and wore a dress or a gown that reached to her feet. She was really pretty, this being of white light. She never looked around, nor at us, but kept her head down and continued her sweeping. She kept up her sweeping until she disappeared.

We returned to the cemetery the next evening and once again we saw the beautiful woman in white. Once again she stood there, sweeping the floor and sidewalk. I don't know but I believe if you go up there, you might very well still see this woman in white and she will stand there, as we saw her, sweeping the floor and sidewalk.

Zanesville's First Burying Ground

North Sixth Street, beyond Market Street was the site of Zanesville's first cemetery, even earlier than the one that lies under the former Pioneer School's playground at the head of Main Street. It became a forgotten burial ground, fairly early in our history.

In 1800, Zanesville had no burying ground. This was shortly to change. In June of 1800, a family was traveling upriver on the Licking River. Caught in a swift current, their canoe upset. All four lives were lost. The parents and daughter were buried on the riverbank and the young child was discovered drowned at Duncan Falls.

John McIntire decided to set aside land on what is now 6th Street for the purpose of burials, including the forlorn family of four. From 1800 to 1806 burials were placed there, though order and record keeping was not a priority. Numerous burials were made, their locations lost. In 1807 some bodies were removed, reburied on Pioneer Hill. Others were apparently left undisturbed. The years passed and they were forgotten.

In 1849, the Zanesville Gas Light Company was organized; the plant was built over and through much of the burying ground. Among the remains that were disturbed were those of a young woman, her red, braided hair still clung to her skull! She was buried just two feet below the ground surface. She received a new grave but how many others didn't? Some believe that part of town continues to be haunted by the spirits of those whose rest was disturbed and denied; all because they were forgotten.

The Fever Plague

The Moxahala Burying Ground was the first site set aside in Putnam for the purpose of serving as a cemetery for early Springfield, called Putnam soon after its settlement. Today when one visits the site, most of the stones are damaged, not legible or simply gone. It is also considered one of the most haunted cemeteries. This story is the first of several that have been presented over the years in our history and from our ghost walks.

In 1809, Zanesville and Putnam had both vied to be the state capital. Zanesville became the capital of the state from 1810-1812. As the government was located in Zanesville, the city grew rapidly and many individuals came to the Zanesville and Putnam area to conduct business. The War of 1812 broke out and this brought more people to the city, including some refugees fleeing the British who initially controlled the great lakes and northern Ohio from Fort Detroit. With all the population movement came disease.

The winter of 1812-1813 was harsh; many people were sickened and suffering. The war wasn't going well and a number of Zanesville area men were in the service, when General Hull surrendered Fort Detroit the past summer and now were prisoners of the British. Stories would be brought into the newspaper offices and this may be how the plague began.

Two men working at the newspaper were sickened with cold chills and then fever. Within only a day or two, both died. News of this went through the community but so did the fever. Several fell sick to the Fever Plague or Cold Plague and for nearly all, it was fatal. For fear of the spread of the disease, the bodies were gathered up and placed in a single mass grave as soon as possible. The names of most of the victims were not recorded and since their burial, Moxahala Burying Ground has been said to be haunted. It is hard to imagine the emotional suffering these individuals went through along with the high fever and eventual death each faced. They did not linger long among the living.

Buried Alive

In the days before embalming was practiced, a great fear was to wake up and find you had been buried alive. Confined in a small space, with the air getting hotter and the breathing more difficult many a desperate person would try to escape, and attempt to claw out of the confining last place of rest. Few were ever rescued.

A number of years ago some children were playing in the Moxahala Burying Ground. They ran about until one tripped over a raised mound of dirt. Dirt flew in all directions and a yellowish white object came to the surface. The children looked on in horror as a human skull, mouth gapping, looked back at them.

Did a rodent bring this macabre relic to the surface or did a desperate man just miss escaping the tomb by inches?

Back, possibly at the time of the plague, a stranger came to Putnam. He was tired from his travels, took his evening meal at an old hotel located in Putnam and settled in for the night.

He awakened in the night with a high fever. A doctor was called but by the next day the traveler had died. He was hastily buried the same day. Did he somehow revive? We may never know the answer, but then, graveyards hold many secrets.

Miss Arnold

Miss Arnold grew up in Putnam and had made many friends in her young life. Death came to her as it did so many in those early days of the 1820's. There was a short illness and Miss Arnold was called into the next world. She was soon buried in the Moxahala Burial Ground and left many to mourn her passing. She had lived just outside town and was much loved by all those who knew her. It was a shock when one, hardly a teenager, was called to heaven.

The next morning, mourning turned to rage as her grave was found to be ravaged and her body removed. Shortly thereafter, Dr. Connant's horse handler, an African American named Jake, discovered the girl's body under a pile of hay in the doctor's barn. One of the girl's limbs was protruding from under the hay, as to say, "Help Me." Though threatened by Dr. Connant's medical students, who said the girl would haunt Jake forever, Jake raised the alarm!

The sheriff seized the medical students and hauled them over to the Stone Academy to be questioned. A mob quickly assembled and wanted the students to be handed over to them.

As there was no law on the books for grave robbery, the students were charged with stealing grave cloths, and taken to the county jail for their own protection, as the mob wanted vengeance. Someone apparently paid bail for the students and they vanished from the area. More shocking yet was what was in store for the sheriff when he returned to the barn.

He went to retrieve the poor girl's remains from Connant's barn, so she might be properly reburied. Upon entering the barn, he found no grave cloths, no ice hook which was used to remove her body from the grave and no girl. Miss Arnold's body was never found, and hasn't been to this day.

Some say she was buried in an old coal mine on Putnam Hill. Others claim that her spirit does not rest and haunts the cemetery and the site of the barn where she was placed. Dr. Connant's grave is located in the same cemetery, the Moxahala Burying Ground as was Miss Arnold's grave. His grave has been disturbed twice since his burial, exposed for public viewing. Perhaps he is denied the rest that his students denied Miss Arnold. She may still be searching for that peace, along with others who were moved, or missed or forgotten as the years passed by.

Dr. Fowler's Plunge

The large broken stone that was near an old tree (1998) on the far right of the cemetery near Moxahala Avenue tells of a grim tale, it records the death of Dr. Isaac Fowler.

The Muskingum Valley is known for thick fogs, especially in the fall of the year. Visibility sometimes goes down to near nothing on those nights. It was one of those nights that the young Dr. Fowler was called out to see one of the families he served. It was an emergency, and couldn't wait tell morning and daylight.

He had his horse hitched and set out to see his patient. He rounded the hill and proceeded down West Main Street toward town. He could hardly see the road in front of him but continued at a rapid pass approaching the covered Y Bridge. The next instant there was a loud crash. He had missed the bridge, gone over the bank and was killed instantly, his body found in the river.

Some have said they hear horse hooves and a crash at the bridge as the accident is recreated, a reoccurring haunting, yet others feel he haunts his final resting place, still struggling with what happened to him that night.

An eerie incident occurred when I was taking pictures of the surviving stones at the Moxahala Burial Ground. I was taking black and white photographs and when I got to his stone, I recorded white streaks that looked like water running down the broken stone. I thought not a lot of it, dismissing it as birds roosting there but I went back the next day and there were no streaks. Sometime later, I was again looking at the photographs and came to his stone. There behind the stone was a white reflection on the tree. In it appeared the image of a human face with a dark beard. I have always wondered if I caught the image of the unfortunate doctor that day.

The Lady of Northwood Cemetery

As cemeteries go, Northwood Cemetery in Cambridge is very peaceful, with nice roads winding through it and lots green grass and trees providing shade on hot summer evenings. It is park-like and inviting. Many individuals enjoy walking there and jogging as well. Several have reported a special visitor that seems a bit out of place, but also out to enjoy her evening.

She seems to appear mostly in the summer and is described as a beautiful young woman in a long white dress. She moves effortlessly among the many stones, seeming to glide quietly, really not interacting with any of the other visitors. She does not travel on the winding roads and is sometimes seen briefly at some distance. She seems happy, almost carefree in her own way.

She has become known as the White Lady of Northfield Cemetery. She seems to take in the loveliness of that special time at dusk when the world seems to begin to relax, a moment of magic between day and night.

The Almost Ghost Story

Cemeteries record history in their epitaphs and sometimes ornate carved designs on some of the stones. There are clasped hands, praying hands, doves, lambs, death heads and trees of life. There are angels, Lilies of the Valley and many other symbols along with veterans' markers and flags. It was the last category; veterans' markers and flags that drew the professor to the old cemetery in Guernsey County. She was locating Civil War Veterans' graves.

It was cold and the ground was snow covered early in 1996. The cemetery was in an out of the way place with no houses nearby but there on the far side of the graveyard she saw a veteran's marker.

She noticed the only recent visitors to the old cemetery, by their tracks, were deer. She really wanted to record that grave so she started across the ground. As she started, a cold wind blew across her face.

Next, there was a sickening sound, a dull thud, as the ground under her feet gave way! One of the early, unvaulted graves had collapsed! The professor found herself on the ground and almost buried to her knees in the old grave. She struggled to free herself, but the grave held fast to its new occupant. Finally, with difficulty, she freed herself, minus her boots.

When visiting old graveyards, or doing paranormal investigation, don't go alone. It's safer and more fun if you have a partner.

Chapter 12

Stories and Investigation

In and Beyond the Valley

Ghost stories and paranormal activity can be found at just about every location where you may find yourself. Exploration is half the fun and where possible, historical research is very important. For those wishing to investigate the world of ghosts and the paranormal, you can start with a basic kit. It is good to have a digital voice recorder, a camera and headphones. Keep a record of each experience through your recorder and also write or type the results shortly after you complete an investigation.

You need not purchase much extra equipment unless you desire it though I would recommend an E.M.F. Detector or Gauss Meter. Remember much of what you see on television is dramatized but use caution and respect private property and rules in public areas. Also use respect as you ask questions to collect Electronic Voice Phenomena (E.V.P.s). Respect cemetery regulations and remember it doesn't have to be late night to collect E.V.P.s, in fact some of the first ever recovered were recovered in daylight, and by accident.

Enjoy this chapter and I wish you all the best should you decide to explore the world of ghosts and the paranormal further. There is still a lot to be learned.

The Old Graveyard

Stone Church Road is a very isolated place these days. It is today part of the wildlife area located on and just off of Route 208 in northern Muskingum County. It is reached from Route 208 near Dresden. In recent years the area was the scene of above ground mining activity.

Fogs often rise up off of the Muskingum River and envelop the woods and old cemetery there. The area was never heavily settled and there is a sense of loneliness as one walks in the burial ground and through the sparsely scattered stones. There is also the distinct feeling that there is a presence with you, watching you as you visit this place. Most of the time, it is just a "feeling".

It was near dusk, the last rays of sun could be seen behind the hills and the trees were silhouetted against the sky when a couple pulled up to the old graveyard. They stopped the car and took in the twilight view. It was a beautiful evening to be out, but even as they sat there, a low fog was beginning to form. It floated in bands and crossed the cemetery, at first in wisps, but gradually getting thicker.

Just as they were thinking of heading on their journey home the figure of a man in overhauls and an old checked shirt came out of the woods and made his way toward them. He looked to be older, probably a farmer, with a thick beard and walked with a slow gait.

As he approached the car, the couple wondered who he might be. Was he the caretaker or maybe he was someone that needed help? Maybe he needed a ride back to town? At any rate, he didn't look to be dangerous or threatening. The couple waited to see what he wanted. He was close now, approaching the car door and window. His hand started to move toward them and then, he was gone. What had he wanted? It was past time to go home for the night!

Harley

Recently, I had an English Bull Dog. My daughter and I were very close to this dog. One evening he had a breathing spell and died. He had had two favorite chew toys he always played with in his room and with us. He would wait on us to get home and play. Well, when he died, we buried one of his favorite toys with him. We never found the other one.

We came home one day, about two months after he died and found the floor was wet in the bathroom, the very spot that we always put papers for him to go when he was alive. We thought that was a little creepy. We made it to the living room and found in the middle of the floor, the stuffing out of Harley's lost toy.

My daughter and I were pretty upset about this because we missed Harley a lot. My daughter asked me what was going on. I said I don't know, maybe Harley misses us too.

Ghost Cats and Dogs

In many households, cats and dogs are a part of our families. They make wonderful companions and many refer to the animals as their kids, or fury children or babies. The bond is strong and when a favorite pet is lost, it can be devastating. Do these bonds continue in the next world in some way? Some talk of one day meeting their beloved pet at the "Rainbow Bridge."

Three ghost cats come to mind, two from here in Ohio and another from the Mountains of North Carolina and Georgia. If one stays at the Buxton Inn, in Granville, it is possible you might have a fury companion for the night. A spirit cat is said the roam the halls and enter some of the rooms. I was told another person felt something against them in bed and got up to see a circular depression in the blankets, about the size of a curled up cat.

One of the lighthouses on Lake Erie is supposed to have a cat that stays there. Glimpses of it have been noted over the years. Apparently a lighthouse keeper had a cat that disappeared and was never found until years later when workers remodeling the structure found its mummified remains behind a wall. It is said to roam the old lighthouse to this day.

Yet another story comes from the mountains and is a very old legend told there. Where did it originally come from? It is what is called a "Haint" tale I first saw a version of it in the *Foxfire Series* published by Elliot Wigginton.

A man, traveling, with no place to stay for the night, is offered an abandoned house, but told it is "hainted". It is cold; he moves in for the night and starts a fire in the old fireplace. Round about midnight he starts hearing cats meowing, lots of them. He looks around and there are no cats. He settles down in an old chair by the fire, the meowing continues, he hollars and at that moment a cat with no head jumps from the fire onto his lap!

The man screams and bolts through the door, running as fast and as far as he can. He stops, trying to catch his breath and hears a voice at his feet. "We ran a good race didn't we?" It was that headless cat!

Members of our Spirit 7 Paranormal Investigation Team were invited to investigate the old public school, now a private residence on the old Adamsville Road between Zanesville and the present Adamsville Road. We were welcomed with hospitality by the present owner and we began the investigation. She had recently lost one of her beloved collies, McLaddie and hoped we might make contact with him as a part of the investigation.

We did a number of E.V.P. sessions and found several spiritual guests, possibly including McLaddie. In one of the photographs was an orb, which by itself, would be questionable but with it, was a faint E.V.P., a dog barking. At the same time McLassie, her living collie acted as though she sensed a presence, looking intently at an area where nothing was visible to us. We concluded that McLaddie had probably let us know, he still considered his old house, home.

Dogs and cats seem to be able to possibly observe and sense things we are unable to discern. Therapy dogs show this ability with their owners.

Who's Calling Me

Ghosts and hauntings are often associated with electromagnetic energy. This is why they the presence of spirit energy sometimes sets off Gauss Meters, causing the needles to spike on the scales or light up detectors. Batteries seem to be drained, and electronic equipment affected, even auto focus settings on cameras can fail to function.

Several years ago, a caseworker was making routine stops at various apartments and homes, checking on his clients. He was accompanied on this visit as the client hadn't called in or made an appointment. One never knew what to expect on these visits.

Upon arriving at the apartment, the workers found the client lying on the couch. They spoke to him, no answer. They spoke louder, still no response. With some consternation, they approached the man. He was dead.

As the two workers stood there, almost in a state of shock, the caseworker's cell phone began to ring. What a time for a call, he thought. He reached for his phone; the number came up on the screen. It was a number he was familiar with. It belonged to the man lying dead on the couch! As the caseworker pushed the button to answer and lifted the phone to his ear, he heard only static.

The Close Call

Captain Snake lived at Wakatomika, a Shawnee village near present day Dresden, Ohio. He left the area in 1774 when the village was burnt by Virginians, in retaliation for raids on the border settlements in Pennsylvania and Virginia. His people relocated to western Ohio and he with them.

He was described as a "plain, grave chief of sage appearance," by some who knew him. Others described him as a "mischievous, bloodthirsty chief, always opposed to peace." In later years he was called a "good old man." He lived to be 100 years old by one account and moved to Missouri with his people in 1833.

If old Snake's life appeared to be a contradiction, then why should his death be any different? Not long after Snake reached Missouri, the years took their toll on the old warrior. His health failed and he soon departed for the spirit world.

The body was prepared for burial and soon relatives and friends gathered for a final viewing. The emotions and thoughts were strong as the people remembered Snake's life. Some likely recalled adventures of long ago and others cried. Many may have stood silently, facing death, as they had so many times before, wondering about life in the next world.

Then as the people looked on, Snake rose up! The shock of the onlookers can only be imagined as the aged chief now faced them. He was alive! Snake was back from the land of death. He recovered his health and lived another three years with his people. He passed from this world again in 1838.

What did Snake see in the land beyond this one? Sadly, no record is known to exist, but the old chief probably achieved new honor and status in his tribe. He was among the very few at that time that left this life and then returned.

Rest in Peace

Camp Moores, north of Zanesville, was a popular summer camp for young boys in the 1950's and 1960's. It featured several small cabins, named for Indian tribes, a large cafeteria, craft barn and Nature Den. There was boating, swimming, crafts, games, archery, a shooting range, and nature study. It was later a Grange Camp for both boys and girls and today (2018) I'm told, may soon be sold if fund raising falls short.

Young children came for the day and went home at night. The older children could spend day and night there. One summer, I stayed at the camp for a week. Toward the end of the week we had a special bonfire and spent a night sleeping under the stars.

We were rounded up by our counselors and marched off on a night to remember. We left the camp and walked a short distance up the road. Our party now turned up a little used mostly dirt road. We climbed the hill and soon came to a cleared field and a pile of stacked wood for the bonfire. The counselors told us that just beyond our little clearing was an old somewhat neglected cemetery, and of course it was haunted.

Imagine our faces when the counselors said, "This is where we sleep tonight, no tents, just blankets on the ground." Soon, however, everyone was enjoying the big fire, cooking hot dogs and marshmallows. Next, came the ghost stories!

The only one I still remember today was a tale of a couple who traveled to Africa and brought back a monkey paw. I've heard it, read of it and even seen a movie on television about it. Our tale was different as the couple threw the severed, clawed monkey paw into the Muskingum River, not far from our camp! As we sat and listened, the claw was said to be making its way to our camp. We were "goners!"

It was time to go to sleep and every sound upon that isolated, lonely hill seemed somehow threatening. There was a rustling in the bushes, a moaning in the cemetery, and something crawling through the woods. I knew the kids on the outside of our group were probably finished! I wasn't far from them. Lightning flashed in the distance and someone screamed! The camp almost went into a panic. We huddled under our blankets pretending to sleep, as the counselors made their rounds. "Are you awake?" was the question heard between numerous buddies. We were sure the people back in the cemetery would rise up and soon come for us.

Eventually, toward morning, everyone dozed off. Then there was a drip, drip as something cold hit our faces. It was still dark and we couldn't see anything, but our blankets were wet, mostly with morning dew.

The next instant a rainstorm broke loose and so ended our adventure. Those that slumber on that hill, if indeed they do, probably remember with glee and a little envy, our night that was spent with them. I still wonder if they were ever really there. Camp counselors can, after all, be full of pranks!

Cowee School

It was October in the beautiful mountains of western North Carolina. The autumn colors; beautiful reds, rusts, yellows, oranges and some tinges of purple were blanketing the mountains all around us. We were there at the cabin for the annual Leaf Looker's Rock and Gem Show and to enjoy our second home and seeing friends. North Carolina and the mountains had been a part of my life since my brother and I were kids, coming down with our mom and dad. It had become a welcome part of Missy's life as well.

Fall and Halloween are actively celebrated back in the mountains and there are always plenty of stories, "Haint" tales too. Stories about ghostly figures, animals, cemeteries, witches and other "Boogers" seem to be everywhere.

We were driving back from town one night, on the road that passes Cowee School. The school once served the whole community and today is used as an art colony, with various active studios. It was getting quite dark but there was some dim light on the school grounds. As we came off the curve, facing the school grounds, we noticed some movement on the grounds below.

There, walking the path near a bench was the figure of a woman. She was dressed in a long black dress, possibly mourning cloths with maybe a vail. She was very much alone and payed no attention to us, not a glance, and we were the only car on the road. She seemed absorbed in thought, just slowly walking there.

As we passed I glanced back, but didn't see her. We have wondered to this day just what we saw that night. Still, when we go by the school at night, we look for this lady in black but to this day we have not seen her again.

An Evening in Ireland

It was late in the afternoon when we landed in Shannon, Ireland. The flight seemed like a long one, we were tired, but excited. We went through customs, picked up a rental car and were on our way to Mrs. Daniels' farm. The climate was mild, misty and everything was a luscious green. Along the coast, we were greeted with Palmetto trees (miniature palm trees) and lots of flowers including some of the biggest roses we had ever seen.

Mrs. Daniels farm was a working dairy farm and a bed and breakfast. She had a young woman operate her dairy and do most of the farm duties. We were warmly greeted and set up in our rooms. I was overjoyed that Mrs. Daniels gave us the run of her farm and its one hundred plus acres.

She explained that there were three fairy forts on the property. These were ancient mounds; two with enclosures, like sacred circles and one a long wall. She also told us that these "little people" were full of mischief. The forts were located along a lane in the pasture fields.

It was getting dark and there was a very fine, misty drizzle. Still, I couldn't wait to walk down the lane and see the "forts." I had thoughts of ancient people, Druids, Roman Legions and of course the artifacts they left behind. The very air seemed heavy with the ancient ones.

Dad settled into his room while Missy and I decided to take a romantic walk in the mists of Ireland. It was easy to imagine the mists taking a human form and traveling with us down that ancient lane. We had rounded a curve and paused for just a moment. All of a sudden there was a feeling of not being alone. I sensed a presence.

We stopped and listened in the rapidly diminishing light. From behind us came a sound. It was the steady clomping of marching feet! Not one or two but many marching feet that seemed to be advancing behind us! We could see nothing, and all of a sudden there was a chill. A nervous sensation was passing through us and the marchers seemed ever closer. Clomp, clomp, clomp, on they came!

There was a metallic clanking and then...a moo! The "Bovine Legion" was advancing under the direction of their human leader, toward the milking station for their evening milking. We laughed and moved on toward the long, ancient wall, abode of the fairies, the little people. We were within a few feet of it and stopped. It was too dark now and time to head back to the farmhouse. We took a fleeting look at the ancient mound and turned back.

As we turned, the heavens literally opened an instant deluge of pouring rain! There was no point to rush or run, we were soaked almost instantly. I could imagine our fairy friends giggling behind the protection or their wall. It was a chilly night for a while as the farmhouse used very little heat. Mrs. Daniels probably had a good chuckle at our luck as well.

In the morning, after a fine breakfast, enough for two meals, and after a pause in the rain, I made my way to the nearest fort. Dodging bovine land mines, I made my way to the fort, scaled the wall, and had a feeling of accomplishment as I stood in the midst of the sacred circle. It seemed almost magical to be there, in Ireland, the home of a number of our ancestors.

The rain suddenly kicked up and I beat a hasty retreat! The rest of the trip we had beautiful weather with a few gentle showers. It felt good to be in Ireland.

Dorothy's Ghostly Kin and a Scent of Lavender

Dorothy set off from Zanesville to visit the home of her English friends. They lived in the English countryside, attending a small church there. It was Sunday morning and Dorothy joined them for church.

She was introduced to some of the family's friends at church and soon the processional began. As the music played, her sense of joy and happiness suddenly changed to one of loneliness. With each note, the feeling grew stronger. The music was beautiful but in a sense seemed sad and bittersweet. The composer had been a distant relative of hers but was called "Little Brother" in church.

Little brother got his name because he had five older sisters in his family. He was saddened by the outbreak of World War 1. He wanted to write church music but that would have to wait. He joined the English Army.

It was 1916 and "Little Brother" was shipping off to France. He made a visit to his beloved nanny before he left for war. She put a ring on his finger to remember her by. "If anything happens to me," he told her, "Come and get the ring." He wanted her to be able to wear it and remember him.

Arriving in France, his unit was moved to the front in an attempt to stop the German advance. His unit bravely charged into no man's land and was cut to pieces. Now, in the dark, he was alone and dying of a bullet wound. He could feel his life slipping away.

He felt a light touch on his hand and looking up; there was his loving old nanny. She handed him some paper and told him to write his processional. She bent over and kissed him and was gone.

In the morning, "Little Brother's" body was recovered and with it, sheets of hand written music! A scent of lavender clung to the papers, the same lavender that the old nanny had been so fond of. That same morning, the nanny's sister found her; she had died the same night. In her hand was the ring and a poppy. There to was the scent of lavender.

Dorothy's friends told her that there are quiet times in the church when one can detect the faint scent of lavender, even when no one else has been in the old church. Some ties seem to last through eternity.

Frozen in Time and Place

Are spirits confined not only by time but also by place or even space? Two strange tales from London and the English/ Scottish border region shed some light and rather dark humor on the subject.

In many places the past is buried several inches or several feet below the present surface. Do spirits suffer the same fate? Some may feel they do.

One night in London, England we decided to participate in a London Ghost Walk. We met near the Tower Station on the tube, by a Roman wall and near to the Tower of London. Our tour explored this central part of the city.

On the tour, our guide pointed to a tiny plot of ground. It was an old cemetery site associated with an ancient Catholic Church. Everything had settled in the cemetery and in some cases only the tops of the stones were exposed, the rest, buried in history.

Our guide pointed out that ghostly monks, in black robes, were said to appear in a procession. We were all taking pictures, hoping to catch something as our guide continued. He said that the ground and walkways they once followed were under the present ground surface. Than he mused, "I wonder if only the shoulders and heads would be visible?" We all got a chuckle out of his remark. He seemed to be poking a little fun at his customers.

In 2009 a story came out of the border area of England and Scotland, concerning buried ghosts. A Roman road was being excavated in the basement of a more modern structure. Someone visited the site and reported hearing strange noises in the basement. The visitor claimed to witness a group of Roman soldiers and horses, well half of them at first, until they reached the cleared roadway and fully materialized!

True or not, I don't know. The only similar examples for comparison I can think of are situations where a spirit seems attached to an old space and will not cross into a modern setting. A case in Gettysburg comes to mind, where a soldier will not leave the old section of a house for the new addition. At any rate, it is okay to be skeptical, always ask questions.

Ghosts at Bryan's Place

Bryan's Place, located on North Sixth Street in Zanesville, Ohio, is a wonderful place for lunch and special events. It has a long history in downtown Zanesville. The site of Bryan's Place was once the Doster-Hodge house and was later, in 1927 and for many years, the Y.W.C.A. It featured special classes and opportunities for both women and men. A number of ladies resided there as well, on the second floor. Today it is a restaurant, sometimes used as a comedy club, meeting center and hosts special events. The building also features home décor and furniture, available for purchase.

A few years ago a photographer set up a photo both as part of an event for young people. The photo booth was very popular and people were excited to try it, sometimes crowding as many as they could in the booth for fun group shots. Little did they know, that they were not the only ones enjoying the booth.

A white mist began to form in the pictures. It intensified and then just as quickly was gone. The image, possibly that of a woman, may have been continuing to enjoy her stay at the place she loved. The camera was repeatedly checked for something on the lens but nothing was found, though the misty pictures continued for a time.

Recently, a downtown ghost walk recorded an image and movement in an upstairs window. Someone must have been as curious of us as we were of them, even though no living person was in the building at the time. If you haven't visited this location, make a point to drop in for lunch. Who knows who might decide to have lunch with you? I don't think you will be disappointed with the fare.

Zaks Restaurant - The Perry Wiles Warehouse

Zaks Restaurant has been a part of the dining scene in downtown Zanesville, Ohio since 1977. It is open on Wednesday through Saturday at 5:00 pm for dinner. Located on north Third Street, it was once the Perry Wiles Warehouse, a distribution center for Zanesville. Today the restaurant features a wide array of selections on the menu and at the bar and continues to be known for wonderful Tex/Mex selections too.

We've collected stories about the restaurant over the many years Melissa and I have gone there. When we were a part of S.E.O.P.I. we set up an investigation for the group and it seemed to confirm some of the stories and allowed us to explore each floor including a hidden storage corridor that might play into the time of prohibition. Zaks is an active place in many respects.

The kitchen area seems to be an active place as lights flicker for no reason. Sometimes appliances seem to turn on and off by themselves. If you are getting a little nervous, a calming hand might touch your shoulder. You turn to look, and there is no one there, that you can see anyway.

Another story suggests there was once an elevator accident and sometimes a presence is noted there, silently watching what is going on. When we were investigating the old office area, we noted a presence, believed to be an elderly man, possibly Mr. Wiles.

One of Mr. Wiles' sisters is said to still keep a watch on the building and its customers. She may have been observed, as a faint female image has been noted. So if you are dining on the great food at Zaks, and are touched on the shoulder, don't worry, it is probably Miss Wiles checking up on you.

Ghosts in the Temple

Masons will tell you they are not a secret society but a society with secrets. The beautiful Masonic Temple building in downtown Zanesville, on north Fourth Street, has its secrets too. It is one of the most active buildings and the center of the Art Colony of Zanesville, by the number of studios and shops within its walls.

Opened in 1903, it was a masterpiece in workmanship in every way. It is no wonder so many linger here, some now for more than one hundred years. Stories abound here, most seem to be about spirits who are attached to a building they loved so much in life. On any floor, you may find them, on rare occasions, they have been seen. Just this past summer (2017) a student of mine left my office area for a moment. Upon returning, she asked, "Do you have ghosts in here?" "Why?" I responded, "Did you see something?" "Yes," was her response," An older man was standing against the wall, across the stairway. He had on like an old style dark suit and seemed to be crippled in one leg." When she glanced back his direction, a second or two later, he was gone. I then said "Yes, this is a very active place!"

Another time, after one on the very popular First Friday Art Walks, a mother and her son were standing in the first floor hallway near the front door. The place was by now about empty but they saw a man in old fashioned cloths and a great coat apparently enter the building from the alley, walk across the hall near the Pepsi machine. The mother and son thought maybe he was going to hide back there and wait for the building to be locked. They walked over and looked behind the machine. He was not there and the door back there was locked as well.

Members of our Spirit Seven Paranormal Investigation Team often led limited public investigations of the building in the hours after First Friday. Many of the rooms and studios were still vacant at that time, around 2011-2013. We collected many E.V.P.'s. We would charge $5.00 a person and the donations went to support the building and activities there. During the duration of these investigations, we collected a number of names on the digital recordings. Some of the individuals were: Jay, Jane, Mike, Jean, Peggy, Laura and David. Some made contact with us on numerous occasions. David, an accountant, on the 4th floor was at first hostile but changed over time. He was probably the individual we heard from the most and seems active yet today as do many others.

March 2, 2012

What had started as an after-hours event for First Friday, thought up by Aaron Chandler, had grown over the months. It was a little fundraiser for the building and was encouraged since many of the rooms were yet to be rented out. We offered public ghost investigations and guided guests through the building. Four members of our Spirit 7 group were often a part of the event; Aaron, Erika, Shalene and me. The guests loved the opportunity to participate in a paranormal investigation.

This night was special in a number of ways at the Masonic Temple building. We had twenty guests despite storm warnings. It had been a year since we had started the event. That night we used electro-magnetic pumps in an effort to enhance the gathering of Electronic Voice Phenomena. That was something new for us; however the bigger factor was likely the powerful storm fronts that were passing through our area that night.

The night would become the most active night in the history of the event. The ghosts were talking! We recorded more than forty E.V.P.s that night on our digital recorders. It was the same night that a regular participant in that event, Mary Hull, photographed two spirit children as Aaron read Bible stories in one of the sessions in room 407/408. The children were seated in an inside doorway as if listening to Aaron's stories.

The guests that night were mostly individuals who by now had had some ghost investigation experience with us or otherwise and explored the building in small groups and we did E.V.P. sessions with them throughout the night. It was certainly a night to remember!

What follows is the compilation of the investigation logs of Aaron Chandler and my own work that night. I used a Sony Digital Recorder and Aaron an Olympus Digital Recorder. Each log is as we wrote them up. Aaron was giving a tour through a part of it or relaying information we had collected from the various areas so only made a limited recording. All areas were either unoccupied or in one case, one of our Spirit 7 member's offices. The times are when, in the order of the recordings that incidents occurred. It is so important to type a log of your investigations.

Aaron's Log:

Masonic Temple public hunt; March, first Friday, 2012. Recorded on Olympus digital. Co1-2nd floor,back stairs

2:30 "No" male response after I ask, Are you lonely?

Then-

2:43 "No" female

7:09 "Mike" (?) (old man) after I ask, could you give me your name?

16:44 "Yea" female response, after I ask, Do you consider this place home?

17:20 "Two" male response, after I ask, do you remember this place one hundred years ago?

17:28 "No" (?) male response, after was there a little boy here earlier?

C 02 3rd floor toy room

:48 "Look" female response, after I ask, may I please have your name?

2:44 female voice, after I ask, so what makes you stay in this room?

C 03 5th floor bathroom

6:35 "Freak" male voice (loud and clear!)

By Aaron Chandler

Gary's Log:

Gary's Investigation Log: Sony Track 27

Gary- Was 1910 a significant year for someone?

4:23 EVP- "Nooo" (Probably Female)

Gary- You don't have to come close to us.

5:36 EVP- "Yes" Male

Gary- Any other male?

5:45 EVP- "Yea, Jay" Male

Gary- Is Charles here?

6:18 EVP- "Yea" Male

Gary- What was it like for you in 1910?

6:39 EVP- "Ucky" Male

Gary- Is there anyone here that was present for the dedication of this building?

7:00 EVP- "Steve (Stu?)" Male, faint

Gary- I describe St. John's Day.

7:54 EVP- "John F--- You" Male

Gary- What was the importance of St. John's Day to you?

8:05 EVP- "F--- You" (3 times, fading) Male

Gary- Jean, tell us your last name?

9:53 EVP- "Dunn(?)" Female

Gary- Why do you like my office, did you work there?

10:10 EVP-"Yes" Female

Gary- If there is a lady by the kitchen door, please join us.

10:58 EVP- "Yes" Female

Was there anyone here during the 1913 Flood?

14:06 EVP- "Yes" (Very Faint)

17:07- I notice Tobacco smoke.

Ballroom Session Ends at 24:14 (Total of 12 EVP's)

Sony Track 28- 9:30 PM Room 508

Gary- Any doctors here?

9:20 EVP- "No" (Very Weak, Breath-like)

Gary- If that is you, approach the lights.

13:43 EVP-"Hi...Yea" Male and Female

Gary- Did you ever have to sleep here at night?

15:29 EVP- "Keep Her" Male (May refer to a woman present.)

Guest- Thank you if you have shared anything.

16:29 EVP- "Thank You" Female (Very Faint)

Session Ends- 4 EVP's Collected

Sony Track 29- 9:55 PM Room407/408 High EMF Room- Gary, Mary, Jennifer and I believe Aaron came in later.

2:29- EVP (Male Shout)

3:00- Loud Tap

Gary- Did you have a favorite restaurant?

3:54 EVP-“Yes” Female

4:01 EVP- “I’m sorry sir.” Male

Gary- Did you shop downtown?

4:08 EVP- “Yea” Male

4:15 EVP- “I answered that.” Male (Somewhat Faint)

Gary- Use the magnetic energy in this room to talk to us.

6:55 EVP- “I can’t.” Female (Class One)

We are discussing pictures in the room.

7:16 EVP- “God, don’t say that.” Male?

Gary- I’ve got a little one you can use. (flashlight)

7:37 EVP- “Shhh” Male

EVP- “I’m sorry.” Female

We are in a discussion. A cool breeze crosses my face.

Gary- If you are here, thank you, I appreciate it.

13:28 EVP- “Thanks”

EVP- “Wow” Male (Faint)

Gary- What do you do in this room?

16:56 EVP- “Budget” Male (Faint)

Mary- We like playing games.

17:29 EVP-“Do You” Male (Faint)

17:52- Investigators experiencing coolness.

Gary- Are there any men present with us?

22:10 EVP- “Yes” (Very Faint, Probably Male)

Guest- I’m getting really cold.

22:14 EVP- “That’s Me” (Very Faint)

Guest- I smell cake.

Session ended at 10:20 PM. 15 EVP’s Collected.

Sony Track 30- I set up Sony Handicam with Night Vision, an IR light, Gauss Meter, EMF Meter and a digital recorder in the basement. Another investigation had night vision as well. Everyone remaining in the building assembled in the basement, about 15 individuals, at 11:10 PM. We did one final session, I presented it. We had audio issues due to the elevator generator. Glenna participated in the session as well.

9:16- Coolness experienced.

10:28 EVP- “Mark” (Possible but Unclear)

Gary- Make us aware of your presence.

15:26- Coolness all around me.

15:45- Guest feels a cold breath blown into her ear.

15:58 EVP- (Can’t make it out due to background noise.)

18:11- Mary feels coolness around her.

19:07 EVP- (Female- Same Problem as Above)

Gary- Were you murdered here?

I continued with were you beaten here, were you raped here?

21:42 EVP's- "Yes" "Yes" "Yes" Female (Due to background noise questionable)

22:35 K2 (Gauss Hit)

Gary- When did this happen?

EVP?- "1935" (?)

22:47 K2 (Gauss Hit)

24:10 - We go silent for five minutes.

33:46 K2 (Gauss Hit)

33:50 K2 (Gauss Hit)

These occur while we are wrapping up the investigation.

Mary- Try to tell us goodbye, we'll see you, thanks.

34:00 EVP- "Yes." Female (Class 1)

We were gathered around the meter (4 or 5 of us) so we were blocking much of the noise around the meter and my recorder. She had to be in the middle of us at tight quarters to accomplish that last EVP.

34:17 K2 (Gauss Hits)

Session concluded at 11:40 PM. 6-9 EVP's collected.

Conclusion: This evening was one of the most active evenings I have ever experienced in an investigation. Weather conditions and possibly the Em Pumps contributed to what we recorded. Historical information aided in the investigation as well. Before the last session of the night, the photo of the little girl and boy was captured by Mary Hull in room 407/408. It remains one of the best photographs I have seen on an investigation I have participated in. The Masonic Temple building is certainly one of the most active buildings and offers many possible opportunities for future exploration.

Pranks a Plenty

There is a classroom area located on the third floor of our building that over the past year has had a number of unusual occurrences that can't be easily explained. Young children, some with special needs, are taught and tutored there. Their presence seems to have caught the attention of some of the temple's ghostly inhabitants. It began last year (2017) and has continued up to the present day.

One of the boys in the class mentioned that he has seen a little boy and that his friend comes to school. The same child noted a little girl in the building as well. This was unusual but only the beginning. As if to make sure everyone knew someone had joined the class, the word "child" began to show up on the microwave screen. This began to happen on a regular basis. Sometimes at school during the day but also when the teacher was arriving to start the day.

I was to witness the word on the screen as well and now that event was joined by yet another. The handprints of a child were noted one morning on the floor, near the door as if someone was playing there. This was a concern as they hadn't been there before and no one should have access to the school rooms. We decided to put down some fine powder near the entrance on the inside of the room so we would know if someone entered it without permission. No tracks were found in the powder but the word "child" reoccurred.

This activity seemed to cease and things seemed quiet. That was until May and June of this year (2018). It seems the ghostly inhabitants have gone from using the microwave and floor to greeting their teacher with loud radio music! The radio was turned off but on more than one occasion now, it has been turned on, with the volume so fired up, it can be heard throughout the halls of the building! It seems like the temple's kids have found a new toy. The radio was unplugged recently and so far the kids haven't figured out to plug it in.

This room was once the studio of Weller artist, Karl Kappes. We once asked if he was putting the kids up to pranks. An older male answered, "Yes".

Mollie's Rock P. 12

(Gary Felumlee, 2018)

Dudley Woodbridge Warehouse and Old Hotel - Marietta, Ohio P.17

(Gary Felumlee, 2018)

James Madison School, Zanesville- Ghostly Children Reported By Entrance P.45

(Gary Felumlee, 2018)

Stone Church Road Cemetery- Dresden, Ohio P.151

(Gary Felumlee, 2018)

Ghostly Image, from the Masonic Temple Building P.164 (Gary Felumlee, 2018)

Ghostly Children at the Old Masonic Temple Building P.165 (Mary Hull, 2012)

A New Beginning- June 19, 2018

Ghosts seem to be always with us, perhaps more popular today than they were twenty years ago when ***Ghosts in the Valley*** was first published. There have been so many experiences and investigations in that time span and yet much still remains to be found. Equipment has changed as have methods but the quest for knowledge continues.

Keep searching the historic record, the oral histories and legends. Talk to those who feel they have experienced the paranormal in their lives. There is a wealth of information there. If the reader desires to record and experience this subject matter, there are numerous resources available. Get some experience with investigators and always record your experiences and observations. Don't go out for just a thrill or to provoke but to communicate. Most investigations are not as dramatic as what we are accustomed to on television or even online. However, it is rare to have an investigation that produces nothing of interest. Personally, I find the more research you do on a site in advance, the higher the level of paranormal activity you might expect.

To start, get a digital voice recorder and have a camera. Night vision equipment is good as are K2 (Gauss) meters, temperature gauges and really at least a second digital voice recorder. Electronic Voice Phenomena (E.V.P.) can be collected night or day though generally there are less background issues at night.

Always get permission before investigating private property and pay close attention to safety issues. It is good to have light sources and a way to communicate. Always follow rules if you choose to investigate any cemeteries. Most post visiting hours from dawn to dusk and battlefields usually have posted hours if they are part of a park system. If you can't or don't wish to visit sites in the evening, early morning can be excellent. Actually the first known E.V.P.s, were recorded in early morning as the individual was attempting to record bird calls!

Our Spirit 7 Paranormal Investigation Team continues work as a group and as individuals. Investigation remains our main focus and we will continue to work with other teams and individuals as we explore the world of the paranormal. We have accumulated information, much of which has yet to be published. There is much yet to be found along the dark paths, lonely roads and forgotten places of our past. As investigators, we can shed light on a subject once feared, hidden away and denied. Do ghosts exist? Each person must form their own opinion. We have collected much information up to this date and much more is out there waiting to be found. Reader, where do you go from here? It is your choice, may your journey be filled with many blessings and enlightenment.   Gary Felumlee, 2018

ACKNOWLEDGMENTS

Many individuals helped shape the direction of this publication by sharing their experiences and participating in so many investigations. Much has been added in the last twenty years to our knowledge on the subject.

First I wish to thank my wife Melissa for sharing this adventure, her encouragement and participation has always been a big part of the project. Next it is important to recognize members of our Spirit 7 Paranormal Investigation Team, past and present: Aaron Chandler, Ashley Dingey, Aaron Felumlee, Keith Felumlee, Melissa Felumlee, Shalene Gates and Erica Talbot. They are pretty amazing. I would also like to thank the members of the Southeastern Ohio Paranormal Investigators, the first group Melissa and I joined, after beginning our own investigations. We have enjoyed working with other groups around the state and numerous individuals throughout our own ghostly adventures.

At Gettysburg we got to know Patty O'Day. Her work and that of Mark Nesbitt have always been an inspiration. Closer to home, Chris Woodyard and all the work she has done over the years, stands out and is much appreciated. I would be amiss not to recognize the assistance and encouragement of Jeff Carskadden when it comes to publication and manuscripts.

Finally, there are so many individuals who contributed stories, shared experiences, or made suggestions toward the content of this publication. The list is long and probably not entirely complete but you are all appreciated for helping to make this collection what it is. A few have left us but all are remembered and thank you.

Kelley Allen, Vicki Hardy Allen, Roger Barons, Marie Bogard, Kristen Leigh Brown, Kay Bunner, Dorothy Bussemer, Brian Bussey, Mona Cantill, Anne Chlovechok, Cheryl Coles, Ann Combs, Tim Combs, Florence Cooper, Frieda Davis, Cassie Dyer, Nola Everly, Keith Felumlee, Lisa Felumlee, Sherry Felumlee, Florence Harris, Bruce Hiestand, Opie Hiestand, Scott Hillis, Jim Hoskinson, Marylyn Hostetler, Renee Huddleston, Chad Hughes, Mary Hull, Dionne Hyson, Jim Kappes, Alice Kirk, Dave Knipe, Mary Knipe, Misty Knox, Cherie Labrun, Jeff Linser, Lucinda Lipps, Wendall Litt, Bonnie Lynn, Lisa Miller, Tonya Metz, Wally Moore, Brittani Mullen, Ron Mullen, Dalia Murray, Ann Nicholas, Jean Norris, Anna Pavlov, Jane Price, Sonya Rambo, Tracy Ray, Joy Rushing, Rose Schmidt, Darla Smith, Marinda Snyder, Phyllis Stevens, Carol Stoneking, Lynne Sturtevant, Joy Talbert, Mitch Taylor and Amy Underwood.

Over the past year, the following individuals have contributed to our understanding of the paranormal through Spirit 7's paranormal investigation work. What you have helped gather should one day lend itself to a publication focused on investigation and what it reveals and adds to our knowledge of paranormal activity. Thank you so much.

Kristen Leigh Brown, Jeff Carter, Cheryl Coles, Keli Crumbaker, Andrea Finan, Morgan Langsdorf, Kevin Oswald, Sherri Oswald, Glenna Rhinebarger and Kelly Sims.

Finally, thanks to everyone who has attended our ghost walks and special investigation activity. Your energy and enthusiasm is greatly appreciated.

Gary Felumlee, 2018

Appendix One: Recommended Readings

Today we have numerous online opportunities for paranormal investigators, including many pages on Facebook and other forms of social media. Our Spirit 7 Paranormal Investigation Team posts on my Gary's Paranormal Crossroads page on Facebook. Some of the E.V.P.'s available for your listening pleasure, relate to stories and locations in this publication. Beyond electronic media, a number of books are recommended for your consideration. These are but a few of what's out there but I have found them valuable and here is a short list.

Lloyd Auerbach's *E.S.P. Hauntings and Poltergeists, (1986)*

Hans Holzer's *America's Restless Ghosts, (1993)*

Mark Nesbitt's*The Ghosthunter's Field Guide to Gettysburg and Beyond, (2005)*

Nancy Roberts's *Appalachian Ghosts (1978)*

Lynne Sturtevant's *Haunted Marietta, History and Mystery, (2010)*

Elliot Wiggenton's *Foxfire 2, (1973)*

Chris Woodyard's *Spooky Ohio (1995)*

Other sources are important for historical research opportunities. Some can be found online. These include the Church of Jesus Christ and Later Day Saints (Mormon Church) and Ancestry. Com. The Mormon Church maintains a large genealogy library and access is free. Ancestry.Com, besides genealogical records, maintains a large collection of old newspapers that can be valuable. I would recommend a membership there if you plan to do research. County courthouse records are helpful as well.

Talk to older members of your community, they are a good resource for tips on haunted sites and stories. Always take notes or use your digital recorder to store information. At any rate, have fun; collecting the stories can be habit forming!

Appendix Two: Sensitives

Sensitives can play an important role in any paranormal investigation. According to Webster's American Dictionary, the word sensitive is defined as; 1.subject to excitation by or responsive to stimuli. The sensitive individual is believed to be able to pick up on the presence of the spirit world. Such an individual often will note emotion and in some cases describe what they see in great detail.

The challenge to using the information gathered by the sensitive individual is validity. There are excellent examples of the work of sensitive individuals but also, unfortunately some very bad examples. It is an area that needs further study and verification. Some confirmation can certainly be found in paranormal investigation and recording electronic voice phenomena, (E.V.P.).

An example of verification comes from an investigation done at Prospect Place at Trinway, Ohio, near Dresden. Melissa and I were a part of the Southeastern Ohio Paranormal Investigators team at that time and we were gathered together in an upstairs bedroom. One of the sensitive individuals picked up on the presence of a little girl in the room. The question was asked, "Is there a little girl with us?" A very polite little voice answered, "Yes, mam." Our digital recorder confirmed the response.

One of the challenges in investigating a site, as to verification, is what information is shared with the sensitive. The investigating team might wish to do a walk through with the sensitive and record what the individual picks up on before sharing much information. E.V.P.'s will often confirm information and on rare occasions you may get photographic evidence.

An effective sensitive individual can be invaluable in directing the investigation toward paranormal activity that is occurring at a specific location. Confirmation through other methods is essential to gain acceptance.

Appendix Three: Investigation Form-Permission to Copy

Site Location ______________________________ Date ____________

______________________________ Start Time ________

______________________________ End Time ________

Weather Conditions ______________________________

Equipment ______________________________

____

Individual Incidents:

Time/Incident ______________________________

Time/Incident ______________________________

Time/Incident ______________________________

Time/Incident ______________________________

Time/Incident ______________________________

Time/Incident ______________________________

Remarks:

References Cited

Anonymous

1881 Bakersville Ghost. *The Coshocton Age.*

January 1, Coshocton, Ohio.

Anonymous

1889 Departed Spirits. *Democratic Standard,*

February 1, Coshocton, Ohio.

Anonymous

1890 Ghost Tale. *Belmont Chronicle*

May 15, St. Clairsville, Ohio.

Carskadden, Jeff

1984 *Famous Railroad Bridges of Muskingum County.*

The Muskingum Valley Archaeological Survey, Zanesville, Ohio.

Carskadden, Jeff and James Morton

1997 *Where the Frolics and War Dances are Held.*

Gateway Press, Baltimore, Maryland.

Felumlee, Gary

1992 *Oratory and Religion, A Recipe for Riot.*

The Pioneer and Historical Society of Muskingum County,

Zanesville, Ohio.

1995 *Putnam Ghost Walk.* Unpublished manuscript.

1997 *James Madison Mourning Theatre.* Unpublished manuscript.

Felumlee, Gary

1998 *Ghosts in the Valley; Ghost Lore of Muskingum, Morgan, Coshocton, Guernsey and Tuscarawas Counties, Ohio* . Gateway Press Inc. Baltimore, Maryland.

2009 *Public Spirits of the Old Putnam District of Zanesville, Ohio.* Privately Printed, Zanesville, Ohio.

Gottfried, Bradley M.

2007 *The Maps of Gettysburg.* Savas Beatie, New York.

Kaufman, Paul

1973 *Indian Lore of the Muskingum Headwaters of Ohio.* Privately Printed, Millersburg, Ohio.

Nesbitt, Mark

2005 *The Ghost Hunter's Field Guide to Gettysburg and Beyond.* Second Chance Publications, Gettysburg, Pennsylvania.

Schneider, Norris F.

1950 *Y Bridge City.* World Publishing Company, Cleveland, Ohio.

1976 Legends. *Times Recorder.* March 21, Zanesville, Ohio

1976 Witches. *Times Recorder.* October 31, Zanesville, Ohio.

1978 Ghosts at the Walter Fye Farm. *Times Recorder.* April 9, Zanesville, Ohio.

Wolfe, William G.

1943 *Stories of Guernsey County, Ohio, History of an Average Ohio*

County. Privately Published, Cambridge, Ohio.

Woodyard, Chris

1994 *Haunted Ohio.* Kestrel Publishing, Beavercreek, Ohio.

(G.Felumlee, 2018)

Downtown Ghost Walk

Story Reference Guide

Photographs - A Fleeting Glimpse

Brafferton Inn; Aaron, Gary, Keith, and Friend! P.38 (M. Felumlee, 2011)

Stone Academy, Mr. McHenry has a friend! In Portrait ! (G. Felumlee, 2017)

Spirit 7 P.I.T. 2012: Erica, Aaron, Shalene, Missy, Gary at Zaks

Parting Shot, (G. Felumlee, 2018)

99260845R00121

Made in the USA
Lexington, KY
16 September 2018